Law of
Attraction
for
Business

How to create a business or attract a job you
LOVE

By Rebecca Hanson

Published by Rebecca Hanson
Victoria, BC, Canada

Publisher: Rebecca Hanson
Illustrations: Raymond Brown
Cover art: Kelly Hewkin, Intuitive Graphic Design
Layout: Neil Sawatsky, appEYEd mediaArts
Editing: Maria Lironi, Cat's-Paw Communications
Proofreading: Carolyn Bateman, Carolyn Bateman Communications
Author's photograph: Frances Litman Photography

ISBN: 4-ISBN0-9735052-0-6

Contact information:
Rebecca Hanson
#110 — 777 Fort St.
Victoria, BC, Canada
V8W 1G9

rebecca@youcanhaveitall.com

Printed in Canada

Table of Contents

Foreword 5

Acknowledgments 6

Testimonials 7

Chapter 1
You Can Have It All 9
Is the universal Law of Attraction a new idea?........................... 10
What's the scientific explanation for how the
Law of Attraction works?... 11
How is the Law of Attraction different
from "positive thinking?" 12

Chapter 2
Your Internal Meter 25
We attract through our vibrations 26
Every subject has a wide range of frequencies........................... 27

Chapter 3
The Law of Attraction Formula 33
The Law of Attraction T-Tool™ for clarity 34
The three phrases for raising vibrations 40
Allow what you've asked for to arrive 45
Anyone can attract a job they love 49

Chapter 4
Become a Powerful Magnet 55
How do we become aligned like a magnet?.............................. 56
A model for a major career transition 60

Chapter 5
Making Your Dream Career come True 67
Five stages of self-actualization 67
What does it look like to actualize a sustainable business? 78

Continued

Chapter 6
    Scripting: The Law of Attraction Business Plan...................... 83
    Components of a powerful script... 86
    EXERCISE: A script template... 87

Chapter 7
    Contrast and Resistance: Change and Growth Motivators ... 95
    Contrast is essential. 95
    Resistance slows the flow.. 96

Chapter 8
    A Guarantee for Success.. 107
    Celebrate each step along the way 108
    Money follows joy.. 114

Chapter 9
    Working in Harmony 117
    Communication is at the heart of every
    good relationship... 117
    The agenda is a vital communication tool in business................. 120
    Core values help make relationships harmonious 123
    Five common questions.. 127

Chapter 10
    Putting It All Together 133
    This could happen to you... 135

Appendix A
Elevations® Skills Assessment... 140

Appendix B
Understanding the Four Communication Styles 149

Recommended Resources.. 162

About the Author 166

Glossary 167

Frequently Asked Questions 170

Book Orders.. 175

Foreword
by Michael J. Losier

A very powerful force, one that you're probably not aware of, is at work in your life right now. It's called the Law of Attraction, and at this very moment it's attracting jobs, clients, suppliers, mentors, relationships, and situations to your life—some good and some not. Rebecca Hanson's book will show you how this universal law affects your career and how understanding its principles can bring you the business or job you've always dreamed of. You'll also gain the necessary tools to use this new knowledge to your advantage.

Using the Law of Attraction, Rebecca and I have worked together since 1999 building a profitable company, TeleClass International Services Inc., and its three subsidiary companies: Telephone Bridge Services, TeleClass Registration Systems, and Corporate TeleLeader Training. During our time in business, perfect clients and suppliers have simply arrived at our doorstep, ideal opportunities have unfolded at our feet, and innovative ideas that stimulated our business's growth just seemed to appear from nowhere. In short, our business has grown steadily from an idea into a successful expanding corporation. All of this is happening because Rebecca and I understand the power of the Law of Attraction and how to use it to benefit our businesses.

In this book, Rebecca shares the secrets and insights we used and, in fact, continue to use to build a company we love. I encourage you to choose this non-traditional approach to get what you want, too. You'll be glad you did.

Michael J. Losier is co-owner of TeleClass International Services Inc., a Law of Attraction coach and practitioner, and author of *Law of Attraction: The Science of Attracting More of What You Want and Less of What You Don't*.

Acknowledgments

I'd like to express my heartfelt thanks to everyone who contributed to the writing of this book.

Thanks to my:

Business partner and friend, Michael J. Losier, who introduced me to this new framework of thought.

Students, clients, and teachers who participated with me in lessons along the way.

Readers who shared their valuable time and honest responses to the early editions of this work.

Storytellers who allowed me to share their stories.

Many editors and coaches who refused to let me be less than I am.

Graphic artists, designers, and illustrators who adorned my written words in beautiful attire.

Favorite retreat center, Dunsmuir Lodge, for providing the perfect luxurious space where I could write.

Special Appreciation

Many of the concepts in this book come from Esther and Jerry Hicks of Abraham-Hicks Publications. It is with lifelong appreciation that I thank them for sharing their knowledge of the Law of Attraction with the world and with me. My life is fuller and richer because of it.

For more information about the Law of Attraction, visit Abraham-Hicks Publications at www.abraham-hicks.com.

Testimonials:

I had to see some evidence to believe it would work for me. I needed to see someone who lived and practiced the way of life I wanted. Somehow, I was attracted to Rebecca's TeleClasses. Now I've seen first-hand, from Rebecca's stories and optimistic energy, that the life I am looking for is right in front of me. By practicing her methods, doors began to open that I didn't realize existed. Rebecca is the proof I needed.
— Tom O'Conner, real estate developer, Mt. Laurel, NJ, U.S.

Over the years I have committed significant time and energy to my own leadership development as well as others. But Rebecca's coaching took it to a new level. I came away with a new understanding of what is possible and the tools to make it a reality. It was a real breakthrough for me. I consciously use what I learned from Rebecca every day and see the changes in my life already.
— Mimi Frenette, personal and business coach, Durango, CO, U.S.

Although I was a relatively upbeat person, I used to worry a lot. However, since working with Rebecca I have changed my thinking dramatically. Now I intentionally focus on positive things and even closely monitor the type of conversations I engage in and the type of programs I watch on television. Through Rebecca, I have gained a thorough understanding of the Law of Attraction and greater clarity about my business. The result? My business has increased. In fact, people who I've known for awhile are hiring my company to do training processes for their organizations! That never happened until I started working with Rebecca.
— Jatrine Bentsi-Enchill, corporate coach, Matthew, NC, U.S.

My work with Rebecca opened my mind to endless ways of working with the Law of Attraction that I never dreamed were possible! Perhaps the most powerful for me was the contrast-to-clarity work using the Law of Attraction T-Tool™, which felt so easy and effortless. Plus, it's lots of fun. It certainly shifted my perspective on what is possible for me. Thank you, Rebecca!
— Ann Ross, corporate coach, Budleigh Salterton, Devon, U.K.

*This book is dedicated
to my dad, Tom Utley,
my very best friend,
closest confidant, and
the greatest appreciator
I know!*

Chapter 1

You Can Have It All

Everything you've ever hoped for ...

Everything you've ever dreamed of ...

Everything you've ever desired ...

Everything you've ever imagined ...

Can be yours. You can have it all.

In all likelihood, you picked up this book because you're thinking about a change in your career or business. You'd like to find an easier, softer, more natural way to make money, and you'd like to be a whole lot happier doing it. You'd really like to have a career you love.

Perhaps you've picked up this book because you're experiencing a crisis in your life. You may have been laid off because your employer has downsized, or you're sick and tired of the corporate world and want a career that feels more fulfilling. Perhaps a change in marital status has thrust you into a place where you need to make more money.

This book isn't about making $40,000 in two weeks or becoming a millionaire in six months. It isn't about the '80s notion of "having it all," where you're trying to wear so many hats you don't know which one is really you. It's not about compartmentalizing your work from the rest of your life.

This book is about creating a business or having a job that is in complete alignment with who you are and what you enjoy most in life. It's about fully integrating work, play, family, friends, and your overriding life's purpose. It's about how to use a powerful universal law, called the Law of Attraction, to create a career or business you love.

Is the universal Law of Attraction a new idea?

Wise men and sages have known about this universal law for eons. The ancient Egyptians and Greeks called it the "Law of Vibration." Other early and present-day scholars call it "Cause and Effect." It's the law of "Sowing and Reaping."

Quantum physics set the scientific community on its ear by suggesting that thoughts affect the outcome of experiments. David Bohm, a noted physicist in the 1980s, explained the phenomena: "Consciousness is much more of the implicate order than is matter ... Yet at a deeper level matter and consciousness are actually inseparable and interwoven just as the computer game, the player, and the screen are united by participation in common loops."[1]

During the early 1900s, the Law of Attraction was rediscovered by people such as William Walter Atkinson, who wrote *Thought Vibration or the Law of Attraction in the Thought World* (1906) and Wallace D. Wattles, who wrote *The Science of Getting Rich* (1910).

Today, the Law of Attraction is becoming more of an everyday commodity. It's the topic of many television and radio talk shows, and people are chatting about it with friends and co-workers.

What is the Law of Attraction?

Simply stated:

> *The Law of Attraction tells us that we become a magnet for whatever we give our attention to— whether it's wanted or unwanted.*

By understanding how the Law of Attraction works, we can begin to deliberately attract more of what we want and less of what we don't want. By *briefly* examining the events that displease us, we can determine precisely what we want. Clear thoughts and statements about what we want draw those people, events, and opportunities into our lives, thus bringing us joy and fulfillment.

What's the scientific explanation for how the Law of Attraction works?

Everything that exists vibrates. On a subatomic level, the protons and neutrons (elements of the atom) are really microscopic packets of energy bursts. These energy bursts keep the atoms in a state of constant motion (vibration), although we can see this movement only through the most powerful microscope.

Our thoughts contain energy (vibrations). The effects of our thoughts can be observed in the following ways:

In our body: Our thoughts evoke certain emotions that cause glands to secrete chemicals or hormones. These cause us to feel either good or bad.

In our environment: Our thoughts send vibrational signals into the atmosphere, much like radio signals, which draw to us people, events, opportunities, and things that match the vibrational frequency of our thoughts.

How is the Law of Attraction different from "positive thinking?"

While "positive thinking" focuses on only positive things, the Law of Attraction encourages us to examine events that feel negative for several reasons:

The negative feeling lets us know that something we are thinking about or observing is not in alignment with our desire.

Ignoring negative feelings doesn't really change our vibration—we are still offering a negative vibration, even when we're not paying attention. This usually causes the negative event to increase in intensity until we *must* give it attention.

Describing what is bothering you, and writing it down, then deciding what you would rather experience, changes negative feelings into positive desires, allowing you to offer a purer positive vibration.

A subtle shift can lead to a whole new way of thinking.

All it takes is a series of subtle shifts in the way we think or feel to easily begin to attract more of what we want. It could be as simple as switching the dial on your radio from jazz on 98.5 to classical on 99.3.

*A series of subtle
shifts add up to
a "paradigm shift,"
a change from
one way of thinking
to another.*

A subtle shift could occur by writing a list, or placing objects that symbolize your desire in your living space to help keep your focus positive. It may be a powerful insight or an "a-ha" moment that alters the way you perceive an event. A series of subtle shifts add up to a "paradigm shift," a change from one way of thinking to another.

If you're a seeker of truth and study philosophy or religion as I do, the Law of Attraction can be the key that makes everything click into place.

Are you ready to learn a new way of living?

Unprecedented stress in the workplace is preparing millions of people to look for a better, gentler, softer, easier way to live.

If you are one of the 40 million American adults[2] suffering from stress or stress-related illnesses, you're probably more than ready to learn a new way of living.

Traditionally, stress is defined as:

The adverse reaction people have to excessive pressure. It isn't a disease. But if stress is intense and goes on for some time, it can lead to mental and physical ill health (e.g., depression, nervous breakdown, heart disease). [3]

It's important for our health, both physically and spiritually, to have work that we love, that truly fulfills us, gives us a sense of purpose, and uses those gifts and talents that truly distinguish us from others.

According to a 1999 U.S. Surgeon General's report, lost productivity and absenteeism due to untreated mental health disorders (with stress as the leading cause) cost American businesses $70 billion annually. [4]

From my personal experience with prolonged stress, I would suggest that the "excessive pressure," to which we react, comes from within ourselves. When we are performing tasks we don't like, or we force ourselves to work in a situation that feels hopeless, we put extraordinary pressure on ourselves to do the impossible. My most serious burnout occurred after years of relentless, round-the-clock motherhood—caring for our five children, two of whom have special needs. My daughter Sarah has Down's syndrome and my adopted son Matthew is autistic and also has Down's syndrome. Since my husband's career as a physician kept him away from home most of the time, I was the primary caregiver. I needed a "stress leave," but how could I have taken one when I was caring for family members?

Eventually, my children grew up and began lives of their own. I was proud of the years I had spent as a wife, mother, and caregiver but now it was my turn to discover what life had to offer me, and what I had to offer it. My husband and I divorced and I began a journey of exploration that would lead me into a fascinating career in information technology. Two years later, I would learn about the Law of Attraction through a new friend. I have not experienced burnout since I applied the Law of Attraction to my life, and my stress-induced fibromyalgia has almost been completely reversed.

It was stress, however, that made me willing to try the Law of Attraction.

I first learned about the Law of Attraction because of a crisis that occurred in 1999 as I was establishing my web design business. I attracted a client (I'll call him David) who very much wanted me to partner in his—potentially lucrative—business.

We began working together on a trial basis. David was a very driven man and he really needed to have a team of people working with him. However, he was reluctant to let go of any aspect of his business, so while I started out as his webmaster, I was becoming something of a secretary. He worked from his home on the east coast of the United States, while I worked from my home in central Canada. The fact that we both worked from our homes and were perfectionists meant we did not have regular business hours. Soon, I was doing things for David that had nothing to do with my passion for web design, but which promised to provide for my future financial needs. I tried my best to be all he wanted me to be, but I was feeling the effects of stress (overwhelmed, frustrated, and exhausted) about once a month. The third time this happened, I asked David for two weeks off from all communication, thinking that a break from his intense energy would give me time to make up my mind about whether I actually wanted to have a business relationship with him.

I wondered:

What should I do? Should I go ahead and go into partnership with him? But what if I keep burning out? I don't think I have the strength for this. If I walk away, will I miss my golden opportunity?

These questions cycled through my mind. But at the end of two weeks, I was no closer to making a decision. So I decided to get away from it all by leaving the city for a brief stay at a bed-and-breakfast.

The hour's drive out of the city, though normally relaxing, barely took the edge off my tension. The quaint little B & B, set on the crest of a hill overlooking a spring-fed lake, was full of "old world charm" with lovely antique furniture, plenty of wainscoting, and period wallpaper. Despite my lovely surroundings, everything felt unfamiliar to me and my room seemed cramped. Someone had been smoking in the house and the cigarette smoke irritated my throat and disturbed my rest. I'd planned to sleep a lot that weekend, but I woke up often during the night in turmoil. On the last night there, I was tossing and turning between my luscious 400 thread-count Egyptian cotton sheets—still uncertain about why I felt so stressed out and no closer to an answer about going into business with David. In the dark, I searched for a pen and wrote this on a little slip of paper:

I need a new framework from which to make decisions. This one doesn't work any more.

When morning finally came, I gave up trying to figure out what to do. I had only a few hours left before checkout time at the B & B, so I decided to listen to a cassette tape a new friend, Michael Losier, had sent me. I'd just tossed the tape into my suitcase at the last minute and not given it a single thought until right then. It was a teaching tape and the subject was the Law of Attraction. Coming from a very religious background, I would normally be leery of listening to that sort of message, but since my old framework had not provided me with the help I needed, I plugged the tape into my cassette player and listened with an open mind. What I heard resonated with me:

If it feels good, it is. If it doesn't feel good, it isn't.

I recognized this as a simple, clear, and clean way to make decisions. This was the new framework I'd asked for and it helped me make a decision about working with David.

Working with David felt like trying to harness a tornado. His ideas were both numerous and scattered—and completely unfocused. Trying to follow his thinking and find a thread that made sense to me was an impossible task and I was worn out. Frankly, it didn't feel good working with him. As I decided I would not become his business partner, I noticed an immediate release of tension from my body. I could breathe easier and my stomach relaxed. Then I wondered if I could continue to work with him in some smaller capacity. But since I seemed to have no boundaries with this fellow, it felt better to sever the relationship than try to tame it.

The message I heard on that tape also advised me to make a list of everything I did want in a business partner. My list looked like this:

I want a ***true partnership*** where …

- Everything is shared 50-50 (the good times and the hard times).

If it feels good, it is.

If it doesn't feel good, it isn't.

- I am treated as an equal.

- I have the freedom to use and develop my gifts and talents.

- We both honor and respect each other.

Eventually, the list grew longer, but it was a start in the right direction. And I did attract such a partner—Michael Losier—the friend who had introduced me to the Law of Attraction by sending me the cassette tape.

Michael and I first met when he did a search on the Internet for "TeleClasses" (classes conducted using a telephone bridge system) and "Canada." My name was the only one that came up on the search engine. Michael had just discovered how easily he could reach a broader audience through teaching TeleClasses. He liked this new distance educational format, yet he felt as if he was the only Canadian teaching this way. Once he connected with me, we started pooling our talents—his for leading TeleClasses and mine for developing websites. In 1999, we started our business as TeleClass Canada. Soon, so many Americans wanted to do business with us that we decided to change the name to TeleClass International. We incorporated the company in 2002.

It took a lot of years of stress and disappointment in my old belief system to prepare me for this new way of thinking. How ready are you?

What would it look like or feel like for you to have it all?

What if *having it all* meant you could have every aspect of your life the way you want it to be? What if instead of trying

EXERCISE: Having it all

Lay this book down for a few minutes and make yourself comfortable. Fix yourself a cup of coffee or tea and put on some gentle, relaxing music. Using the exercise below or your journal to write in, complete this sentence: "If I had it all, I would have (be, see, feel, do, hear, taste and smell)." Use all your senses to imagine what your life would be like if you *had it all*.

"If I had it all, I would have ...

"I would be ...

"I would see ...

"I would feel ...

"I would do ...

"I would hear ...

"I would taste ...

"I would smell ...

"In short, I would ...

to please your boss, your spouse, your children, the creditors, and anyone else who wants a piece of your life, you could live in a way that honors who you are, respects your likes and dislikes, fosters your personal growth, and provides all the means with which to do so? Would a life like that feel as if you *had it all*? I asked a former client and a student to share how it would look or feel if they *had it all*.

Peggy, a TeleClass student wrote: "If I had it all, I would be doing everything in alignment with my values and priorities. I would have the time to be there for my children. I would bring to my counseling and coaching clients an inner peace and presence, unencumbered by financial or practical concerns. I would live in an environment ideal to my family's needs and lifestyle. I would feel secure, peaceful and able to experience the joy of life every day. Hey, you know what? I'm getting real close to this."

Jen, a coaching client said: "If I had it my way, I would feel free to pursue my life purpose without anxiety about money. I would work in an environment that focuses on wellness rather than sickness. My supervisors and co-workers would look for the good in others. I would enjoy my work and feel as if I were contributing to the well-being of this planet instead of fixing what's wrong with people.

"I would take time to enjoy some finer things in life, such as traveling to Fiji or Japan. I would take up golf or bowling and not take myself so seriously. I might even sign up on one of those dating services and have some fun trying to find the man of my dreams. If I had it all, I would be very grateful for what the past had taught me, be thankful for what I have now, and look forward to the future."

Regardless of how you arrived at this place at this time, you're about to find what you've been looking for. The answer is here—simple and clear: **Through understanding and applying the Law of Attraction, you *can have it all*.**

It's never too late to become what you might have been.

—George Eliot, historian

Summary

The Law of Attraction provides you with a simple, clear, and clean way to make decisions based on what feels good. Ultimately, harnessing the power of this universal law will allow you to have every aspect of your life the way you want it to be.

....

1 Will Keepin, "Lifework of David Bohm: River of Truth," http://www.vision.net.au/~apaterson/science/david_bohm.htm.

2 Lori Widmer, "A Not-So-Hidden Workplace Cost," *Risk and Insurance* (July 2002). Also available online at http://articles.findarticles.com/p/articles/mi_m0BJK/is_8_13/ai_89018208/print.

3 Health and Safety Executive, *Work Related Stress*, a downloadable pamphlet, http://www.hse.gov.uk/pubns/indg281.pdf.

4 ibid, Widmer

Being attentive to your feelings is the first step toward discovering a life you love.

Chapter 2

Your Internal Meter

Life presents us with endless choices. Daily we ask ourselves questions about our livelihoods, often feeling hopeless about finding answers.

However, each of us is created with an internal meter for knowing whether something is right for us. That meter monitors our emotions and feelings.

> *Positive emotions feel good.*
> *Negative emotions feel bad.*
> *If it feels good, it is. If it doesn't feel good, it isn't.*

This is such a refreshing way to know if something is right *for you*.

We all come from different backgrounds and have observed different approaches to life. I was raised in an environment where emotions and feelings were not to be trusted. I believed what I was taught—that if you acted in the *right* way, good feelings would follow. But most of the time, I would be disappointed. Even though I went against what felt right *to me* and did what *others told me was right,* those joyous emotions never arrived.

Do good feelings and happy, joyous emotions result from doing the right thing? The truth is that every person has a meter that is individually calibrated for specific purposes. *Your meter is for you.* It's in alignment with all you were created to be and do.

When you're feeling good, happy, joyful, and positive, you're in alignment with all you were created to be and do; you send strong vibrational signals into the atmosphere. These signals attract more positive situations so you can feel even more wonderful.

> *Like attracts like.*
> *Positive feelings attract positive events.*
> *Negative feelings attract negative events.*

We attract through our vibrations.

It's easy to tell when someone is in a bad mood. We know how it feels when we're close to them or talking to them. Often we want to stay away. When someone is in a good mood, it feels good to be around him or her. In both cases, we're feeling vibrations.

Your thoughts, feelings, emotions, and moods (positive and negative) send a range of vibrations into the atmosphere. These vibrations act like big magnets and attract, draw, or pull in to you the people, events, opportunities, etc. that are a "vibrational match" to the vibrations you're emitting.

Can we see these vibrations? No. They're more like sound waves. Here's an example of how these invisible vibrations attract:

You've probably heard of a dog whistle. It's a special metal whistle that summons dogs. It sends into the atmosphere a vibration that humans can't hear. When you first blow into it, you may think that it hasn't made a sound. That's because your ears can't tune-in to the frequency or pitch, but dogs hear the sound and they come running toward it. The presence of the dogs is proof that the sound was made.

The Law of Attraction works the same way. Our thoughts create an emotion that sends out a vibration. The Law of Attraction responds to this by sending us experiences that match the vibration.

If we give a lot of attention to a situation that feels good, we give off positive vibrations and attract more situations that are positive.

If, however, we give a lot of attention to a situation that doesn't feel good—a situation that makes us feel angry, afraid, upset, or disappointed—then we emit negative vibrations. They will attract more negative situations into our lives.

There's one more thing for you to know about vibrations.

Every subject has a wide range of frequencies.

When I gave the illustration of the dog whistle and you pictured dogs showing up, did you feel excited or pleased to think of dogs coming toward you? If you did, then the subject of dogs is a high-frequency subject for you. For me, the thought of dogs showing up evokes a feeling of fear and I want to run. For me, the subject of dogs is a low-frequency vibration.

High-frequency subjects feel good.
Low-frequency subjects feel bad.

The Law of Attraction responds to the *sum total of your vibrations* at any given time. So if you want to feel good, then keep your thoughts focused on subjects that feel good. If you want to attract more pleasurable experiences into your life, then notice, appreciate, and celebrate everything you enjoy. The idea is to develop an abundance of positive emotions from which you'll attract more of what you want in life.

My father is the most appreciative person I know. A while ago, he was visiting me and seemed very interested in learning about the Law of Attraction.

While we were out shopping, I insisted upon stopping at one place and then another and another, searching for a metal counter. It's one of those devices that you *click* to keep track of the number of items you're counting. People counting stock in a store often use them. Finally, I found one. When we got into the car, my dad looked quite bewildered and asked, "What are you going to do with that?"

I replied, "Do you remember that double rainbow we saw this morning? Well, [*click, click*]."

"And do you remember how the sun was shining while it rained and the rain looked like silver tinsel? Well, [*click, click*]."

My dad caught on right away. For the rest of his visit, whenever either of us appreciated something, we'd say, "You'd better give that a *click*."

Each time we gave something a click we would laugh, or smile and joke about how many clicks we had gathered that day. People watching us may have wondered why we were so happy. We were giddy with joy.

One afternoon, my dad began to talk about an unpleasant memory. As I tuned into his vibration, he stopped me and said, "We'd better drop this subject or we'll lose two clicks." We laughed as we realized how a simple little metal counter could raise our vibration so wonderfully that we dared not lose a single click.

The best way to break a habit is to drop it.

You can use an "Appreciation Counter" to help notice the abundance of beauty and the wealth of goodness already in your life. Just purchase a counter from a toy or stationery store and see how many clicks you can get in a day. Notice the shift in your feelings and emotions when you deliberately appreciate what is working well in your life.

Now that you know a little more about the Law of Attraction, I'm going to show you how to harness the power of this law to make it work *for* you rather than against you. The key is in knowing how to apply the Law of Attraction formula.

> *Our feelings are our most genuine paths to knowledge.*
>
> — Audre Lorde, feminist and poet

Summary

Each of us has an internal meter for knowing whether something is right for us. It monitors our emotions and feelings and tells us whether we're feeling good or bad. When we feel happy, joyful, and positive, we're in alignment with all we were created to be and do; we send strong vibrational signals into the atmosphere. These signals attract more positive situations so that we can feel even more terrific. However, because the Law of Attraction responds to the sum total of our vibrations at any given time, it's important to keep our thoughts focused on subjects that feel good.

Our thoughts today create tomorrow.

Chapter 3:

The Law of Attraction Formula

The definition of the Law of Attraction is simple:

We become a magnet for whatever we give our attention to—whether wanted or unwanted.

Attraction works by vibration. We vibrate through our:

- Thoughts
- Emotions
- Feelings
- Moods

Whatever we *think* about causes an *emotion* that feels either good or bad. The sum of our *feelings* creates the *mood* that sets the frequency of the vibrations we're emitting. These vibrations enter the atmosphere and, like a magnet, pull into our lives more experiences that match our overall vibrational frequency.

Most of the time, we're unaware of our vibrations. We react to daily situations in the moment and pay little attention to whether our vibrations are positive or negative.

Now we've decided to be *more aware* of our vibrations because we've learned that if we're not conscious of what we're vibrating, we'll keep attracting a jumbled assortment of experiences. I call this awareness "deliberate attraction."

Deliberate Attraction is a simple, three-step process through which the Law of Attraction delivers your desired experience.

Step A: Get clarity about the outcome you desire.

Step B: Raise your vibration to match your desire.

Step C: Allow what you've asked for to arrive.

Step A: Get clarity about the outcome you desire.

How can you become clear about what you *do* want? Here's a guaranteed way:

> **Examine *briefly* what you don't want for the purpose of becoming clear about what you *do* want.**

Describe, by putting into words, what does *not* feel good. When you *briefly* examine a subject that doesn't feel good with the intention of changing it, then you're actually *clearing away* an unwanted vibration and *replacing* it with a wanted vibration. ("Briefly" is the amount of time it takes you to notice something doesn't feel good. For some people, "briefly" may be only a few seconds; for others, this process could take a few days.)

The Law of Attraction T-Tool™ for clarity

Here's a tool you can use to help you replace unwanted feelings or events with wanted ones. I call this the Law of Attraction T-Tool™. One is provided on the right, or you can make your own. Here's how:

1. On a blank sheet of paper, draw a large letter "T" down the middle.

2. Choose a topic about which you need to become clear.

Law of Attraction

T-TOOL™

Contrast

I don't want ...

Clarity

I do want ...

Law of Attraction T-Tool™
Topic

	I don't want ...	I do want ...
1.		
2.		
3.		
4.		
5.		

3. Label the left column *I don't want ...* and the right column: *I do want ...*

4. Begin on the left side and write down everything you don't want to experience. For example, take an aspect of your business or workplace and write down the things that aren't working well. If you've worked in several different places, think about the last three or four and write down everything you didn't like. (Remember to examine each item briefly—you don't have to relive it, just put it into words.)

5. Next, carefully examine each item in the *I don't want ...* column and ask your Inner Being this question: "So if I don't want this, what do I want?" (Your Inner Being is the unseen spark of divine life within you. It is your True Self, Pure Love, Goodness, God, Universe, or Spirit within.)

6. Write what you do want in the right-hand column using the corresponding number from the left column.

Formula for Desired Experience

$$A + B + C = DE$$

(Desired Experience)

7. Now, fold the paper down the middle so the *I do want…* list is facing you. Crease the paper firmly a couple of times. (How does it feel to be done with those things you didn't enjoy?)

8. Keep the Law of Attraction T-Tool™ handy with the *I do want…* column facing you. You'll need it for Step B.

Getting clarity: Valerie's story

Here's a real-life example of how one businesswoman used the Law of Attraction T-Tool™ to attract her ideal job.

For Valerie, a Toronto real estate agent, business was flat. She hadn't attracted any listings or sales for some time and was running out of money. She needed a job and she didn't want to leave the real estate field so she decided to become an assistant to an agent. A week after our coaching began she had already had four job interviews and identified seven *non-negotiable* items. To help her get even more clarity about attracting her ideal job, she decided to make this Law of Attraction T-Tool™ while she continued booking more appointments. *(See table at right)*

"Each appointment brought me more clarity, and I was able to get a clearer picture of what I *did* want," writes Valerie. "Within a month, I'd spoken to a dozen real estate agents in Toronto. Visiting so many offices and speaking with so many people in the industry really raised my vibration. I began to believe I *could* attract precisely what I wanted in a job."

Law of Attraction T-Tool™
Topic: Real Estate Career

I don't want ...	*I do want ...*
1. To receive commission only	To receive salary plus commission or bonus
2. To lose my realtor's license	To retain my independent contractor status
3. To lose the chance to sell when I get a referral	To retain all my clients, contacts, and any referrals from these sources
4. To drive very far to work	To work in an office located in the center of this city
5. To work with people who fail to disclose all I need to know	To work with people who are easy to communicate with and approachable
6. To work with a boss who is so disorganized she can't find her desk	To work with a boss who is well-organized
7. To work 24/7	To work a reasonable amount of hours

Step B: Raise your vibration to match your desire.

Have you tried using affirmations and found they didn't work for you? They never worked for me either. I would write out an affirmation about how I had this and that as if I had it already, but something inside me would shout, "No you don't." I have a strong sense of truth and I don't feel good telling myself things I don't really believe. Because it's important to stay true to myself, I created three phrases that raise my vibration bit by bit. I use them in conjunction with the *I do want ...* list.

The three phrases for raising vibrations incrementally are:

Phrase 1: I'm in the process of attracting my ideal ...

Phrase 2: The Law of Attraction (or God, or Providence, or the Universe) is in the process of ...

Phrase 3: I love it when ...

Here's how to use the three phrases to raise your vibration for attracting anything—including a career you love:

Phrase 1: I'm in the process of attracting my ideal ...

This phrase is true because as soon as you begin to look at what you *do* want, you've *begun* the process of attracting your desires.

Using the first phrase, along with her Law of Attraction T-Tool™, Valerie began speaking about her ideal workplace like this:

I'm in the process of attracting my ideal job where I receive salary plus commission or bonus.

I'm in the process of attracting my ideal workplace where I can retain my independent contractor status, all my clients, contacts, and any referrals from these sources.

I'm in the process of attracting my ideal workplace, which is located in the center of this city.

Once you begin to get clarity, you are in a process.

I'm in the process of attracting my ideal boss, someone who is easy to communicate with, approachable, and organized.

I'm in the process of attracting my ideal new job where I can work a reasonable amount of hours.

Each time Valerie repeated one of these sentences, she could feel her vibration getting higher. Her energy and her mood improved as well. Her whole outlook on life brightened. If she found herself sliding back into the *I don't want ...* column, she would catch herself and say, "The truth is (because it is the truth) I am in the process of attracting my ideal job."

Once you're entirely comfortable talking about your desire using Phrase 1, you can move on to the next phrase:

Phrase 2: The Law of Attraction (or God, or Providence, or the Universe) is in the process of ...

As soon as you become deliberate in aligning your vibrations so all of your thoughts, feelings, and emotions are positive, then you're co-operating with the Law of Attraction instead of resisting it. The Law of Attraction notices that you're sending a clear, strong, positive signal, and it begins arranging all that needs to happen for you to receive your desire.

It took a few weeks before Valerie felt comfortable using the second phrase in combination with her *I do want ...* list:

The Law of Attraction is in the process of bringing to me my ideal job where I receive salary plus commission or bonuses.

The Law of Attraction is in the process of unfolding everything necessary for me to find my ideal workplace where I can retain my independent contractor status, all my clients, contacts, and referrals.

The Law of Attraction is in the process of arranging my ideal workplace where I can work in an office located in the center of this city.

The Law of Attraction is in the process of introducing me to my ideal boss, someone who is easy to communicate with, approachable, and well-organized.

The Law of Attraction is in the process of orchestrating all that I need to know, say, or do to attract my ideal new job, where I can work a reasonable amount of hours.

When you're ready to raise your vibrations to the top of your meter, you'll want to use the third phrase:

Phrase 3: I love it when ...

Close your eyes and imagine yourself in your new workplace. When you're able to see it, feel it, hear it, smell it, and taste it, you'll know with certainty that it's about to be yours.

Valerie's *I love it* list looked like this:

I love it when I receive salary plus commission or bonus.

I love it when I can retain my independent contractor status, all my clients, contacts, and any referrals from these sources.

I love it when I work in an office located in the center of this city.

I love it when my boss is easy to communicate with, approachable, and well-organized.

I love it when I can work a reasonable amount of hours.

EXERCISE: Play the *I love it* ... game

Any time you need a quick boost, play the
I love it ... game.

Sample:

> *I love it* when my clients show up on time.

> *I love it* when my clients have completed all their homework.

> *I love it* when my clients readily surrender their credit card information so I can easily process payments.

> *I love it* when my clients respond to my emails within the same day.

> *I love it* when my bank account balance is going up, up, and up.

> *I love it* when I am able to pay my bills as soon as they come in.

> *I love it* when I can take time off to get my hair done or play golf.

> *I love it* when I can shop for groceries in the middle of the day.

> *I love it* when I can stay in my pajamas until noon because I work at home.

Just a few short minutes of playing the *I love it* game will boost your vibration over the top.

Now that your vibration is soaring, all you have to do is let the Law of Attraction go to work. This takes us to Step C.

Step C: Allow what you've asked for to arrive.

If we could keep our minds and hearts in a state of *allowing* (relaxed, joyful expectation), what we desire would simply show up. Instead, we begin to *resist* our own desires by entertaining *doubtful thoughts* and *fears*. Both are powerful negative emotions that cause resistance and block or delay the reception of what we desire. The poet William Shakespeare wrote: "Our doubts are traitors, and make us lose the good we oft might win, by fearing to attempt."

Most of us are very good at constructing stories that support our *doubts* or limiting beliefs.

"It might happen for others, but it never does for me."

"Every time I think I'm getting a promotion, it slips through my fingers at the last minute."

"I can't get ahead in this job."

"What if I don't get the raise I asked for?"

"I hope it comes in time. But I doubt it will."

"If I want something very much, I won't get it."

The endless self-talk and stories go on and on. They all contain the same element—doubt. Doubt may be blatant or so subtle its presence can only be felt as a slight tension (resistance) somewhere in your body. Here's where the real work begins.

I usually begin to notice that I have doubt when something I want is slow in showing up. Until I become aware that it hasn't arrived yet, I'm usually oblivious to the doubt. Once I'm aware of doubt, I ask my Inner Being, "What old belief do I have that is causing this doubt?" Sometimes I pray: "I don't know what I need to know, but I need to know it. Send me the answer in a way I'll clearly see or notice."

The answer may come in the form of a new thought, the still small voice of your Inner Being, a sense of knowing, or a feeling. Sometimes the answer comes through watching a movie, reading a book, listening to a tape, or talking with another person. I've even found the answer in the newspaper headlines.

When the answer comes, I ask my Inner Being, "What truth do I need to receive so I can let go of this limiting belief?"

When you ask the question, the answer will come.

When the answer arrives, you'll notice that your body relaxes, you have positive thoughts, you feel confident, and you believe you'll receive your desired objective.

As belief outweighs doubt (you don't need 100 percent belief, just 51 percent), the process of receiving all your goals, desires, and hopes for a joyful business that generates money (or whatever you want in life) will start to become your reality. Just believe that it's possible for you to have what you've asked for. As you stay in the mindset of possibility, certainty will grow. Certainty is the opposite of doubt.

> *The thing always happens that you really believe in;*
> *and the belief in a thing makes it happen.*
> —Frank Lloyd Wright, architect

Fear is another major hindrance to receiving what you want and can be an unrecognized predominant vibration—that is, you may not be aware of a deep-seated, long-standing fear that is vibrating on a subconscious level. The Law of Attraction responds to your fear by orchestrating situations that give you new opportunities to recognize fear and choose a different response.

Let me give you an example where the Law of Attraction gave me another chance to overcome fear.

One day, Michael and I received a threatening letter from a business competitor that was meant to intimidate us. As I read it, I felt the familiar physical sensations of fear: the joints in my body became weak, my stomach felt upset, and it was difficult to think clearly.

Previously, this type of fear would have debilitated me for days. However, this time I remembered that the word fear is actually an acronym (FEAR).

F = False

E = Evidence

A = Appearing

R = Real

My logical mind told me that something in this letter was not true, so I prayed for guidance. Then a clear thought came to me, "Give your lawyer a copy of this letter." The lawyer investigated the competitor's claims and discovered that our company had done no wrong. The threatening letter was just a fishing expedition. Everything was fine.

What this intimidating letter did for me was reveal a deep-seated subconscious fear of losing control over my finances. The Law of Attraction responded to my hidden emotion, exposing it in a way I could not miss.

When fears are exposed, their power is lessened and fear is replaced by confidence.

When doubt is replaced by certainty and fear is overcome by confidence, you will know that whatever you want is on its way.

> *Have a vision not clouded by fear.*
> —Cherokee proverb

Use the three-step Law of Attraction formula to grow your business.

As you start your business, you can use this simple three-step process to achieve clarity, raise your vibration, and receive the perfect associates, tradespeople, and suppliers—whatever you need to grow your business.

During TeleClass International's first year of business, Michael and I realized that neither of us wanted to do the bookkeeping. It wasn't our area of expertise and we needed someone to guide us. We used the Law of Attraction T-Tool™ to determine what we wanted in a bookkeeper:

- A mature person
- Years of experience in bookkeeping
- Available right away
- Able to quickly comprehend our business in order to set up the books
- Computer savvy
- Affordable

About an hour after creating our *I do want …* list, I phoned Michael back with the good news that I knew someone who fit our description—my dad. He was retired. He had spent more than 30 years as a financial comptroller, bookkeeper, etc. for companies of various sizes. He was computer savvy enough to have created the software used in the payroll departments of two large hospitals. And he wouldn't charge us much for his services. My dad was the *perfect* person to help us get started, and he was delighted to work with us. Often, when we get clarity about what we want or need, we recognize it sitting right there at our elbow.

Anyone can attract a job they love.

One day, my daughter Sarah, who has Down's syndrome, announced that she was going to send her résumé out again.

"Why, Sarah?" I was quite surprised. "You have a good job right now as a custodian in a government building. Why do you want a different job?"

"I'm bored," she replied, "I want a change of scenery and I want to do lots of things, not just one thing over and over."

A week later, Sarah's supervisor asked if she would accept a transfer to another job location. He thought she would be happier working with the custodial crew at a small private college. For Sarah the new position was made to order. She was getting just what she wanted: a change in location and the chance to perform a variety of tasks and work with different people in a lovely environment.

While others may have viewed her disability and said to her "You're lucky to have a job at all," Sarah wasn't satisfied with a boring repetitive job. She was perfectly clear about what she wanted and was so confident that she could attract another job that she did! And finding a better job wasn't difficult. Once Sarah set her intention and was *willing* to do the legwork, the Law of Attraction took over and arranged everything.

But that wasn't the first time my "disabled" daughter has used the Law of Attraction to get what she wanted. Sarah used the same combination of clarity, desire, and confidence to meet her lifelong sports hero, hockey star Wayne Gretzky. She also used it to ensure that she made a TV appearance during a local festival and had an opportunity to take professional-quality photographs of the Queen of England—but those are stories for another book.

Remember, deliberate attraction is a simple, three-step process:

Step A: Get clarity about the outcome you desire.

Step B: Raise your vibration to match your desire.

Step C: Allow what you've asked for to arrive.

Formula for Desired Experience:

A + B + C = DE (Desired Experience)

As you become more confident in the Law of Attraction's ability to deliver your heart's desires, your doubts and fears will take a back seat. Confidence and joyful certainty will become your predominant vibrations. What you need or want shows up quickly and easily.

The degree to which you are *certain* of your desire is an indicator of the degree to which you are *allowing* all the goodness of life to flow to and through you.

Ask, and it will be given to you; seek, and you will find; knock, and it will be opened to you.

—Matthew 7:7

Summary

There are three easy steps to making the Law of Attraction work *for* you. The first step is to become clear about what you want in your life by *briefly* examining what you don't want. You can do this by using the Law of Attraction T-Tool™. Then raise your vibration by incorporating the three phrases "I'm in the process of … ," "The Law of Attraction is in the process of … ," and "I love it when …" Finally, replace doubts and fears with certainty and confidence and you will receive your desire.

Now that we know about the Law of Attraction formula and how to use it, the next step is learning how to increase its power.

Like attracts like.
Positive feelings
attract positive
events.
Negative feelings
attract negative
events.

Chapter 4

Become a Powerful Magnet

Do you know why one piece of steel becomes a powerful magnet while another piece is simply an ordinary lump of steel? In an ordinary lump of steel, the positive- and negative-charged atoms are going in a hodgepodge of directions. The magnetized steel, however, has had its atoms lined up so that all its positively charged atoms face one direction and all its negatively charged atoms face the opposite direction. This alignment of atoms is what transforms ordinary steel into an attracting magnet. How does this alignment occur? One way is to place ordinary steel in close proximity to a lodestone, one of Earth's natural magnets. The lodestone's strongly polarized atoms have a polarizing effect on nearby steel.

Most of us, like the ordinary lump of steel, are sending mixed messages to the Law of Attraction because we're confused about who we truly are and what's important to us. We feel uncertain about our purpose in this life. We say one thing but believe another.

For example, if I say that I want my web design clients to pay a deposit in advance for my services, yet I doubt that they will, then I am sending mixed messages and the Law of Attraction is receiving two conflicting signals. One signal says, "Send clients who will pay a deposit" while a second signal says, "I'm not capable (or worthy) of getting a deposit from my clients."

How do we become aligned like a magnet?

If we want to become powerful magnets, attracting more of what we enjoy into our lives, then we'll want to have clear, positive, good feelings about ourselves. We can discover who we are and what we truly love by noticing what feels good. Then we can begin to accept ourselves with our personal set of preferences and act in ways that honor our core values. Core values are deeply embedded values that give us guidance by producing good feelings when we honor them and negative feelings when we don't. Honesty, kindness, loyalty, compassion, and goodness are all core values.

When I first started my web design business, I struggled with the fact that I knew no other women in Saskatoon, Saskatchewan, who were interested in the Internet. This vocation was clearly a masculine domain. Some of my friends were afraid of the Internet and I had to make a choice—join them in their unfounded fears or stand up for myself and what I loved doing. I chose to honor myself by learning how to create websites and starting my web design business. In doing so, I demonstrated my growing sense of self-worth. I was aligning my life with who I am—a wonderfully creative person!

One of my coaching clients recently learned this same lesson: That it's important to make decisions that are in alignment with one's core values.

My client's business was at a standstill, and she was feeling fearful about not having enough money. She had recently purchased some equipment at an electronics store, then had found the exact same item on sale at another store and bought it as well, planning to return the first one. However, when she examined the sale item, she discovered it had a flaw. Now she had a dilemma. She wanted to keep the unflawed item, but she wanted to pay the sale price. In her desperation over money, she decided to get her money back from the first store by substituting the flawed item from the second store.

This act of dishonesty caused her to feel badly about herself. She noticed the bad feelings and knew they came from her dishonesty, but she convinced herself it was too late to set the record straight. This only compounded her negative feelings and vibrations.

No wonder she couldn't attract into her life the business she wanted. Her first negative feeling, fear around not having enough money, actually set her up for the next negative choice—dishonesty. This in turn set her up for more negative feelings of embarrassment and fear of reprisal.

When the pain of all this negativity was too much, she began to say things like: "I really don't like what I just did. I want to feel good! What shall I do to help myself feel better?"

Within a few minutes, she had an opportunity to make choices and take actions that could either honor her core value of honesty or dishonor it some more. She wrote me about her experience:

I was feeling pretty bad when I returned to my office, and then remembered I needed to go to the bank. I went up to the bank *machine and there was $40.00 sitting in the slot that the previous customer forgot to take. I took it out of the machine and put the money in my pocket while I did my own banking.*

Now I was dealing with the moral dilemma of what I should do with the found money. I so badly wanted to keep the money as I am heavily in debt with all my credit cards almost maxed out.

I decided to leave the $40.00 with a teller at the bank. I'm glad I did. I am feeling much better!

I feel like the Universe gave me an opportunity not only to redeem myself, but also an opportunity to change my vibration after doing something about which I felt badly.

Here's another example of how the Law of Attraction responds to one's own magnetism.

TeleClass student Jacquie Fox realized that not being financially responsible was creating a negative vibration that affected her new business. Once she decided to act responsibly in the area of her finances she became a powerful magnet for money! She wrote me this humorous letter about how the Law of Attraction helped her pay off her debt faster than she could lose 20 pounds.

I have always believed that losing weight is "easy" because it's all in my control, while eliminating a $20,000 debt is "difficult" because it's not in my control.

Well, amazingly, my debt is paid and my weight has not budged—except perhaps in the wrong direction.

By September 2001, I'd been out of work for one year, accumulating debt on numerous credit cards, and not wanting to face the reality of what I owed. At the end of that month I landed a part-time job.

Around November or December 2001, I finally decided to face my debt head-on. It was $20,000. I was asking my Inner Being for guidance, and I received the idea to consolidate the debt from five credit cards into one. Several months later I found an interest-free card, so I switched the balance over to that card and began paying just over the minimum payment each month.

As quickly as I could, I began paying at least $200 over the minimum payment and some months I could pay as much as $1,000.

Then, in September 2002, I discovered the Law of Attraction and began working with it. Soon, there came a "knowing" inside of me that my debt was handled—I didn't even have to think about it anymore.

By January 2003, my debt was down to $12,000. At the end of that month, I received an unexpected inheritance, which allowed me to pay off all my debts and go on a cruise with my husband.

Now, here I am, still struggling with those 20 pounds. What I thought was not in my control somehow happened easily and effortlessly. What I thought was in my control, seems not. So, now I'm going to apply the Law of Attraction to losing weight. Really I am.

Jacquie's story demonstrates a wonderful truth. Once we are in alignment with our true self and core values, everything we need or want (money, opportunities, supplies, or help) can come from unexpected sources. We don't have to know how a solution will show up or from where it will come, we just need to set our intention to line up our thoughts, actions, and beliefs to the place where we feel very good about ourselves.

As we become more and more aligned with who we are, *based on what feels good*, we begin to notice that we're becoming powerful magnets. We're attracting whatever we need to know, say, or do. More of our endeavors are successful and bring us joy.

Just as ordinary lumps of steel need to be close to a lodestone to become powerfully magnetic, we need to surround ourselves with others who are in alignment. When we are in the company of these "human lodestones," our own magnetism is strengthened. This is one of the most noticeable benefits of having a coach who lives the Law of Attraction. The Law of Attraction practitioner has her own life in alignment, and people who get close to her will notice that her magnetism has a positive effect on their lives too.

A model for a major career transition

What happens when we realize we need to make a major life change, such as finding or creating a new job, in order to be true to ourselves? I've coached some people who decided to walk away from their jobs. While it felt like the only way to get free from a job they hated, it didn't afford them the *feeling of safety* from which to grow or create a healthy new business. The lack of a regular paycheck created a fear of financial ruin, which was evidenced by mounting debts.

Abundance can't be created in an atmosphere of neediness. Abundance flows when we feel safe.

My business partner, Michael Losier, is a good role model for how to maintain a positive vibration while carrying out a career transition.

Michael was a consultant for the government of British Columbia when we first met and began our business, TeleClass International. His passion was teaching classes on a variety of topics by telephone and training others to do the same. In the start-up phase, all the money we earned went back into the business. It took almost a year before we were able to regularly pay ourselves a little bit each month. As the monthly amount increased, Michael cut back his hours with the government to four days per week. Although this was something that had never been done before in this department, his employer agreed to let him do it. Later, he asked if he could work only three days a week and again received what he asked for. Finally, the day came when it *felt safe* for Michael to quit his government job. It was a day filled with joy and celebration, with the fear around finances notably absent.

If you are aware of your need for a major career change, here are some suggestions for ways to maintain a sense of safety and abundance while making that change:

1. **Retirement pay:** Some companies are eager to offer early retirement packages, which can support you while creating a business or looking for a job that is in alignment with who you are.

2. **Spousal support after a divorce:** I was able to start my own businesses with a sense of safety while receiving spousal support.

3. **Inheritance:** An unexpected (or expected) abundance of money can suddenly set you free to change careers.

4. **Any part-time job that will pay for the basics of life:** What are you willing to do while creating your dream job?

5. **Disability benefit or insurance claim for personal injury:** One of my friends used her time recovering from an accident to become clear about her core values and to learn how to honor them through her business.

6. **Workers' compensation:** Stress or medical leave is a great time to realign with your core values.

7. **Move in with parents one more time:** If Mom and Dad will take you in!

8. **Angel investors:** Don't be surprised if some people believe in you enough to support you financially while you build your dream.

9. **Increase or expand your skills:** What do you enjoy doing? Do you lack the skills to do it? How about getting a student loan while studying something you really love?

10. **Multiple streams of income:** Look for more than one way to receive money. Could you do this *and* that?

11. **Obtain a loan:** New business start-ups often qualify for loans or government grants.

12. **Sell things (on eBay, on consignment, at garage sales):** Your castaway items may be valuable to someone else.

13. **Home equity:** Visit your bank or mortgage broker to see if your home can act as your safety net during this time of transition.

14. **Savings:** If you have at least two years' worth of income plus additional money for business start-up costs, you have the freedom to work on your new business full-time without having another income.

A safety net will help you maintain positive vibrations around money while you're creating a new business or career.

Being in alignment with your core values and feeling safe are fundamental to allowing all that you desire to become your reality.

Man is a magnet, and every line and dot and detail of his experiences come by his own attraction.

— Elizabeth Towne, author, *The Life Power and How to Use It*

Summary

As we become more aligned with who we are and our life's purpose, based on what feels good, we become powerful magnets. We attract everything we need to know, say, or do. Each of our endeavors is successful and brings us joy. Similarly, when we surround ourselves with others who are also in alignment, our own magnetism is strengthened. But anytime we do something that isn't in alignment with our core values, we experience negative emotions that hinder us from receiving the real desires of our heart.

*The answers are
all within you.
Listen carefully.*

Chapter 5

Making Your Dream Career Come True

Finding a business, job, or career that fulfills your life's purpose is a very exhilarating discovery. Although career aspirations are only one facet of a full life, feeling you are making a contribution to the world can influence other aspects of your life as well: social, spiritual, intimate relationships, and family. Happy, fulfilled people tend to make better community members, better parents, better friends, and better spouses. They are people who feel at one with themselves. Psychologist Abraham Maslow, one of the founders of humanistic psychology, called this being self-actualized: "A musician must make music, an artist must paint, a poet must write, if he's to be at peace with himself. What a man can be, he must be. This is the need we may call self-actualization. It refers to man's desire for fulfillment, namely to the tendency for him to actually become what he is potentially: to become everything that one is capable of becoming."[1]

One day I discovered that I could use the Law of Attraction to simplify my own self-actualization. I noticed there are five stages that I go through to achieve this level of authenticity.

Five Stages of Self-Actualization

Stage 1: Know yourself

Stage 2: Accept yourself

Stage 3: Honor yourself

Stage 4: Trust yourself

Stage 5: Love yourself

Then I realized that my businesses go through these five developmental stages with me. As I develop and mature, so do my businesses.

Stage 1: Know yourself

Get to know what you love. Clarity is the first step in the Law of Attraction formula. Close your eyes and ask yourself:

"What would I rather be doing right now?"

"If I could do anything I want, what would that be?"

Wait patiently for the answer. You may see a picture in your mind, notice a thought, hear a word, or experience a feeling.

Think about the following statement in terms of attracting your ideal business or job:

"What I'd really love to be doing right now is ...

_____

_____."

Did you write something? Take a few moments to do so. This is the first stage of actualizing a sustainable business or job that you love.

Knowing yourself: Karen's story

Karen Krueger is a busy mom of two-year-old twins. She asked me to help give her coaching practice a boost. Karen is very intuitive and connects easily with people and animals. She was writing résumés at the time we started working together, so her answer to my question of what she'd rather be doing right now if she could do anything she wanted, came as a sweet surprise.

"I would rather be in the barn with my horses," said Karen. "Lucy has been sick ever since we moved here and she really needs my attention. I love my horses and I really miss being with them."

Then I asked Karen to do something I'd never thought of doing with a client before. I asked her if she would try an experiment with me. She agreed and I led her into a deep energetic connection with her sick horse (through stillness, deep breathing, and envisioning her horse). During this guided connection, she tuned into Lucy's energy and diagnosed the problem.

The shift in Karen's vibration was obvious to both of us. She sounded excited and relieved to have an answer—not just to Lucy's illness but also to her own lack of vibrancy. She gave herself permission to spend time with her horses. Karen could hardly wait to get off the phone.

It turns out that Karen has always loved working with horses. She remembered that she had already been using Reiki and other energy-shifting techniques successfully on horses. She is, in fact, an intuitive, energetic healer of horses. Recently, Karen ordered a homeopathic treatment for her horses. She received more validation of her gift for intuitive healing when Obie, her oldest horse, developed symptoms of West Nile virus. Karen applied the treatments and by the time the lab results confirmed that Obie did indeed have West Nile virus, he was already cured.

Karen is becoming recognized in her community as an excellent, intuitive horse healer who can be called upon to work with a horse that is ill or injured. She's having fun exploring more and more aspects of her intuitive gift, and she's filled with joy to now be doing what she loves.

Is there a business in horse healing? There is if you learn how to know yourself the way Karen did!

How long does it take to reverse a lifetime of negative thinking? The Law of Attraction is not "keeping score" of how long you were thinking negatively. It responds right away to your shift in vibration. How long it will take to notice that the majority of your thoughts are positive is up to you. There is no "standard" amount of time. I think it took me about 18 months to feel as if the majority of my thoughts were more positive than negative—and I was coming from a very, very low vibration.

Although I was trained as a registered nurse, I hadn't worked outside the home in 30 years, and I needed to do something to help support myself. It took a while for the answer to come, but when I got very still inside, the answer came—web design. Although at that time I'd only created one website for myself, I'd truly enjoyed the process. I have a huge creative component within me and it was ready to play. Based on the answer I heard, I taught myself how to develop and design websites. (Years later, I still love web design. It has been the mainstay of my work, and I love getting paid for doing what I love.)

It's refreshing to meet people who define themselves by what they love.

Then, not long after this insight, I woke up with another word emblazoned on my mind: entrepreneur.

It was a message from my Inner Being. It was so clear and specific that it was almost visible. I now own seven Internet-based businesses and love creating Internet businesses for other people.

If you're uncertain about what you want to do, use the Law of Attraction T-Tool™ to help you clarify what elements feel good to you in a business, job, or career. It's amazing how much clarity comes when you begin to make the connection between various situations and how you feel about them.

Spend a few minutes with the Elevations® Skills Assessment found in Appendix A. By sorting through the different skills and assigning them to one of three categories, you can discover which skills you enjoy the most, which skills you feel neutral about, and which ones will likely cause burnout. (You can hire other people to handle those jobs.)

As you get to know yourself, you'll want to move into the next stage.

Stage 2: Accept yourself

While it's one thing to know what you love to do, it's another to *accept* that knowledge and awareness about yourself. One of the greatest hindrances to self-acceptance is repeatedly asking ourselves: "What will people think?" In a family or society where love and acceptance are conditionally based upon behavior or conformity, this question can have a crippling effect.

The Law of Attraction teaches us that we are responsible for what we attract into our lives. My mother isn't responsible for what comes into my life. My church isn't responsible for what I attract to myself. My friends do not set my vibrational frequency. I am responsible for my vibration and my fear of other people's opinions will neutralize my positive vibrations about my business or my life in general.

Acceptance is a decision. I was 50 years old when I decided to form my own opinion about myself. I distinctly remember hearing a church member denounce the Internet as being demonic. I loved the Internet and had to ask myself if I was going to buy into that way of thinking or form my own opinion. I was so hungry for global communication that I was among the first 200 people in Saskatoon, Saskatchewan, to sign up when the Internet arrived in that part of Canada. It was the first time I had formed an opinion that went directly against the opinion of an elder in my community. It took courage to say, "Well, you can think that way if you like, but I love communicating with people around the world."

That decision brought about a huge shift in my perception of life. As I began to take a stand for what I felt was good and right and acceptable to *me*, I noticed I was able to accept other people when their ideas differed from mine. I did lose a few friends, but the satisfaction of self-acceptance far outweighed any short-term sense of loss.

Self-acceptance is simply making one decision after another to accept that what I like is good for me.

Self-knowledge and acceptance lead to action—the third stage in self-actualization.

Stage 3: Honor yourself

We honor who we are by doing things that move us in the direction of our desires. Honoring ourselves raises our vibration to a higher level. When I began honoring myself as a businesswoman and entrepreneur, I joined several local business associations. Each time I introduced myself, I felt more comfortable hearing myself say, "I'm Rebecca Hanson, the owner of Aurora Websites."

If you see yourself as a new business owner, here are some specific actions you can take to honor yourself:

1. Decide on a business name and perform a legal search to see if this name is already registered or if it's available for you to use. (NOTE: I suggest you do this before you register an Internet domain name. I worked backwards when I started my web design business. I was using a domain name that didn't meet the provincial requirements as a business name, so I had to choose a new name for my company and get another domain name, thus wasting time and money.)

2. Register the new business name.

3. Obtain a business license.

4. Open a business bank account.

5. Design and print business cards.

6. Join a professional business association.

7. Research various means of receiving money easily from your customers or clients. Here are a few methods I've used:

   a. Obtain a merchant account so you can accept credit cards.

   b. Open an online account with a business that allows you to accept checks electronically. That way you'll know for sure that the check is in the mail and not sitting on the dashboard of your client's car.

   c. Use a secure Internet site like PayPal.com to accept funds.

8. Write a business plan the Law of Attraction way—as a script. You'll read more about scripts in Chapter 6. For now, just start out with the phrase: "If I had my way…" and write as if your business were in full swing and thriving right now. Imagine how every detail would look, smell, taste, and feel. Keep in mind that the script is a powerful tool and that every detail is important.

If you're looking for a *job* you love, here are some specific actions you can take to honor yourself:

1. Use the Law of Attraction to attract more information about the specific job you desire. Do research into the qualifications, the salary range, and the demand for people who do this job.

2. Visit companies that offer positions you would like to have.

3. Become an expert in some aspect of this job.

4. Have a professional prepare your résumé so it targets the specific job market you desire.

5. Imagine how you'd like to feel while you're working at your ideal job. Now write a script paying careful attention to every detail. (Is your office big and sunny or small and cozy?) Start out with the phrase: "If I had my way, I'd be working as ..." and write as if you were working in that job right now. In Chapter 6, you'll learn more about scripting. Taking actions like these will help you see yourself being, doing, and having your *ideal job.*

Stage 4: Trust yourself

Trust your *inner knowing.* Trust the way each situation feels to you. Trust that the still, small voice you hear, or the picture you see, is true for you. Trust your gut feeling and the joy you feel when something is perfect for you. Trust develops over time and through experience.

A sense of peace within yourself is a good indicator of how much you're *trusting* that what you've asked for is on its way.

Sometimes what we want is delayed for reasons unknown to us. Trusting yourself means following your intuition, sensing peace within yourself, and demonstrating the ability to believe that all really is well even if the outward events haven't yet manifested.

I recall one coaching client who wanted to attract a six-bedroom house for less than $300,000 in a major U.S.

city. She was very clear about what she wanted and why she wanted it. She would consider no less than six bedrooms and would pay no more than $300,000. I worked with her for a month, explaining how the Law of Attraction works; then I sent her off on her own to attract the house. About four months later she sent me an email with 24 photos attached. She was so excited to share with me her joy and that of her family as they explored their brand-new home for the first time! Indeed! She had attracted a brand-new six-bedroom house for less than $300,000. I picked up the phone to congratulate her. As we talked, we realized the house had not yet been built when she first expressed her desire. In fact, it took exactly five months to build the house. This real-life example taught me that delays can occur simply because it takes time to create what you've asked for! And it taught me that even if what you desire doesn't exist, the Law of Attraction will put it in someone's heart or mind to build it for you.

Trust is like a muscle; it develops over time with use.

Stage 5: Love yourself

Loving yourself is the natural outcome of the first four stages of self-actualization. Knowing and accepting yourself, honoring and trusting yourself lead you into loving yourself completely. It's from this place of loving ourselves that we truly vibrate the clearest and purest vibrations, knowing that we fully deserve to receive all that we could think of or ask for. The subject of self-love is so profound, that I need to write another book to describe it in depth. In fact, I have begun to write that book already!

As you move through the five stages of self-actualization using the Law of Attraction, you'll be creating the business, job, or career of your dreams at the same time. You'll be growing in self-knowledge and self-acceptance. You'll make choices and take actions that honor your true self. And you'll grow in confidence and certainty, which translates into a solid, sustainable business that contributes both to your life and the lives of others. The end product is inevitably a career or job you love!

> *Once you have the intention,*
> *the Law of Attraction shapes the experience.*

What does it look like to actualize a sustainable business?

Michael Losier and I have been creating TeleClass International using the Law of Attraction formula and the five stages of actualization. We have successfully grown our business parallel to our individual processes of being true to our core values and self-actualization.

We started the business investing a little bit of our own money plus our time and talents. Since we were both aware of the high value we placed on being financially responsible, we chose to keep our personal debts separate from the company, and rather than incur debt, we used money we made through training TeleLeaders (people who teach over the telephone) to develop every aspect of our business, including the online

TeleClass Catalog registration and administration software. Both Michael and I have other sources of income and feel safe letting TeleClass International grow itself.

We started with an idea and followed the Law of Attraction to create an actual company that makes more money every year. We continue to enjoy the natural unfolding of our lives and our business.

Here's how Michael and I actualized our business through the five stages of self-actualization using the Law of Attraction.

Knowing ourselves: We used the Law of Attraction T-Tool™ to clarify each aspect of our company. We made T-Tools on our:

- Ideal clients
- Referrals
- Sales team
- Trainers
- TeleLeaders
- Publicity
- Programmers
- Accountants
- Bookkeepers
- Administrators

We spoke about our company using the three phrases: "We're in the process of ... ," "The Law of Attraction is in the process of ... ," and "We love it when ..." We wrote desire statements and plenty of scripts. We noticed what was not fun and what we loved doing.

Accepting ourselves: We acknowledged to ourselves, and to each other, when we no longer enjoyed doing something. And we celebrated when we discovered something that we loved to do. We accepted each other's strengths, talents, and preferences as being complementary. We celebrated our differences.

Honoring ourselves: We hired other people to do the tasks we no longer enjoyed so we could focus and excel in those parts of the business we loved.

Trusting ourselves: We noticed when something didn't feel right. We have a rule that if one of us doesn't feel good about something—like hiring a consultant or doing a marketing campaign—then it's best to wait. We've learned to trust that our intuition will tell us when something isn't quite in alignment with our highest good.

Loving ourselves: We have both matured to the place where we are comfortable with ourselves and our ability to make choices that honor us. Our companies, then, have become merely reflections of who we are and what we love to do.

TeleClass International is a sustainable business. It has grown in a gradual, natural, solid, reproducible fashion. We've listened to our inner guidance system each step of the way. We've created a business we love and it sustains us.

But what about a business plan? (I can hear someone asking that question right now.) We never did get around to writing a formal business plan (although we came close), but we did write a Law of Attraction business plan—the script.

> *Remember always that you not only have the right to be an individual, you have an obligation to be one.*
> —Eleanor Roosevelt, American First Lady and humanitarian

Summary

Self-actualization is the term psychologist Dr. Abraham Maslow used to describe the process of becoming everything that one is capable of becoming. This process is simplified by using the Law of Attraction. There are five stages you'll pass through on the way to achieving your own fulfillment:

1. Knowing yourself and what you love.

2. Accepting that knowledge because knowledge and acceptance will lead to action.

3. Honoring yourself and what you are becoming.

4. Trusting your inner knowing of yourself.

5. Loving yourself as a whole and complete person.

As you evolve through these stages, so will your business, job, or career.

1 A.H. Maslow, "A Theory of Human Motivation," *Psychological Review* 50 (1943), 370-96. (A summary of Maslow's work on self-actualization can be found at http://www.performance-unlimited.com/samain.htm.)

The act of writing alerts the *Law of Attraction* to the desires of your heart.

Chapter 6

Scripting: The Law of Attraction Business Plan

What is the difference between a business plan and a script?

A formal business plan is a written document outlining a series of logical steps that should rationally lead to the realization of a goal in business. A business plan follows specific guidelines and requires certain information. While it originates from a goal you have in your mind, it follows a format dictated by the experiences of others.

A script, on the other hand, arises from your imagination. You can write what you want and not have to follow guidelines set by someone else.

Imagination is an integral part of our Inner Being, our subconscious mind, and our intuition. When we write a script, a message is conveyed from our Inner Being and brought to our conscious mind in the form of feelings. Our conscious mind then reaches for the words that best describe those feelings. The words are actually symbols of the feelings. The act of writing out the words creates a physical experience that connects our body to our imagination. Seeing the words (symbols) that have been written, or hearing them read aloud, anchors the imaginary experience in our subconscious mind.

The script produces a total body, mind, and soul experience. Scripting accesses all four parts of the brain:

The left brain, which deals with words and logic.

The right brain, which understands patterns and symbols.

The mid-brain, which experiences emotions.

The brain stem, which registers physical stimulation.[1]

When all four parts of the brain are engaged, a powerful message is delivered to the Law of Attraction that puts your plan on autopilot.

If we let go of resistance to this imaginary experience, our subconscious mind will guide us toward its actualization in the easiest, most natural way.

Do we need to know in advance how our script will become our reality? No.

Once the script has been written and the outcome (goal) has been felt, heard, and imagined in this deep way, the Law of Attraction has been activated. If we pay attention to our intuition, or gut feelings, it will guide us to every situation, circumstance, opportunity, or piece of knowledge we need to achieve our goal. Again, having a script is like running on autopilot. Set your destination, then relax and enjoy the ride.

I invite you to write a script about how you want to feel owning and operating your ideal business or working at your ideal job. Close your eyes and imagine yourself opening the office in the morning, putting on the coffee, and checking your email. Imagine how it feels to be interacting with

Writing a script puts your plan on autopilot.

your customers or clients. Are you sitting or standing? What clothes are you wearing? What background sounds do you hear? What's the view outside your office window? Imagine going to the bank with a stack of checks for deposit or viewing your bank account online and feeling that rush of excitement when you see the latest deposits.

Components of a powerful script:

1. The objectives should be clear.

   a. What do you want?
      Set lower limits but not upper ones.
      Example: "I want $10,000 or more."

   b. Why do you want it?
      Example: "I want $10,000 or more so I can purchase the office equipment necessary to start my new business."

   c. How does it feel to have it?
      Example: "I love having $10,000 or more to start my new business. I feel safe and comfortable starting out with enough money to buy equipment and pay my first two months' office rent."

2. Every objective should be believable. If being specific causes you to feel resistance, then pull back and be more general. If it feels better to be specific (about amounts, dates, or details) then stay firm about the specifics. Ask yourself, "Do I believe this could happen?"

EXERCISE: A script template

Here's a script template you can use as a guide to prompt you to describe what you are imagining:

If I had my way ...

I would see ...

I would hear ...

I would feel ...

I would smell ...

I would taste ...

"The Law of Attraction is in the process of orchestrating all I need to know, say, or do so I can easily attract and receive my ideal_____."

3. Every objective should be stated in only the most positive terms.

   Less positive: "I want at least 12 new clients ..."

   More positive: "I want 12 new clients or more ..."

4. The script should start with a statement like:

   "If I had my way ..." or "If I could wave a magic wand ..." or "If I were in charge, I'd ..."

5. End the script with a phrase such as:
   "The Law of Attraction is in the process of orchestrating all I need to know, say, or do so I can easily attract and receive my ideal _____."

I like to end my scripts with this phrase because it helps me let go of figuring out how this will happen and allows the Law of Attraction to bring it about in the very best possible way.

Here's a real-life example of how to use both the Law of Attraction T-Tool™ and scripting tool to attract the perfect job.

Remember Valerie, the realtor who wanted to find a job in real estate that assured her of a salary plus commission? During one of our coaching sessions, she confided to me that she felt some uneasiness around her desire to work reasonable hours. She wasn't sure why she felt this way, so we used the Law of Attraction T-Tool™ to get clarity. First she put into words all the reasons why she didn't want to work 24/7. Then, based on that list, she verbalized what she did want to do with her time.

Law of Attraction T-Tool™
Topic: Real Estate Career

I don't want ...	*I do want ...*
1. To miss running in the morning	To have plenty of time to go running in the morning
2. To miss doing yoga	To stay home and practice yoga
3. To feel like I can't get a haircut when I need one	To have control of my daily schedule so I can get a haircut whenever I choose
4. To feel like I can't have fun with my friends because I'm always on-call	To spend time with my friends—planning social time in advance, knowing that I'm not on-call for work
5. To miss out on time with my family	To be there for my family members when they need me or for important occasions
6. To feel pressured to leave for work so early that I skip my morning meditation	To come into the office after the morning rush traffic

As we wrote this Law of Attraction T-Tool™, Valerie realized what she wanted was plenty of time to take care of herself.

This time she wrote a script about her ideal job and included some important self-care activities. Here's how Valerie's script evolved:

Valerie's script

I wake up at 7 a.m. every morning and go running for 30 minutes and also meditate for 30 minutes. Once a week, when I am doing my yoga routine, I rise at 6:30 a.m. (Points 1 and 2 from Valerie's I do want ... list.)

I have a very flexible schedule, which allows me to avoid the rush-hour traffic and arrive at my office at 9:30 a.m. and leave at 3:30 p.m. If I want to work more hours and earn more commissions, it's my prerogative to work past 3:30 p.m. Also, I have the flexibility to leave at noon if I have a doctor's appointment or want to get my hair cut. I'm in charge of how many hours I work so it's easy to plan my social life and spend time with my family. (Points 3, 4, 5, and 6 from Valerie's I do want ... list.)

My co-workers are cheerful and upbeat. My colleagues are also very honest and have a great sense of integrity. They always disclose important information that I need to know, such as a commission that will be split by us on a referral sale.

My office is neatly organized, which gives my clients a great first impression. All my documents are filed where I can find them in less than 30 seconds.

My workplace allows me to dress in a business-casual fashion, which enables me to be comfortable while doing my job.

On my desk, around my computer, are pictures of my family and friends to remind me that I am loved. I have a coffee mug warmer on my desk as well, which allows me to keep my morning drink perpetually warm.

At one point, Valerie almost accepted a position with a real estate company. After giving it more thought, however, she decided that it was not a precise match for what she wanted. The tone of that company was too competitive, and she would have been expected to live and breathe real estate 24 hours a day. But she never would have been able to identify this without having written her script.

It took courage on her part to decide to wait for the Law of Attraction to line up an ideal career opportunity that matched *all* her desires. It was a decision that paid off handsomely.

I recently met with another real estate agent and I explained to her that because of my debt, I was seeking a partial salary that would allow me to stay in real estate. I told her how I wanted to work as part of a team, especially since the top agents in the city that I compete against all have teams behind them. Therefore, instead of competing on my own as an individual, it would be easier and more profitable to join a team.

She and I then brainstormed about how we could make this work. After a few more meetings, I agreed to move my business over to her small real estate firm.

The terms of our agreement to work together meet all the non-negotiable items from my Law of Attraction T-Tool™:

I retain all my clients and continue practicing real estate.

I receive a small salary in exchange for administering our small office, a responsibility I share with a third agent.

In discussing the time I could start each day, I asked if it would be possible for me to come in at 9:30 a.m. or 9:45 a.m. so

I wouldn't have to fight the traffic. My new partner suggested I could start working at 10:00 a.m.

With three of us working together as a team, we could cover for each other. No one would have to work 24/7 and if someone was sick, one of us could look after the other's clients.

Not only did this working relationship meet all of my non-negotiable items, it also met a lot of the other criteria I'd scripted and written about in my journal.

Rebecca, I got it all!

There's also another level to this story. I learned many things about my own business style and myself during this whole process.

Interviewing so many real estate agents allowed me access to their businesses in a way that I would never have had the opportunity to see otherwise. It made me realize how much business there really is out there.

Now I fully understand that it's my job to let people know about me. I can now see how isolated I was. I realize that I am as good as any other agent, but if no one knows about me, how can they find or choose me?

I realize that I have to be more pro-active in my own business. Every positive step I take opens me up to getting more business. Whether that activity brings an immediate, tangible, positive response isn't as important as the way it makes me feel by raising my vibration, which opens me up to even more business.

Money is an exchange of energy and money comes from people. Therefore, the more people I connect to, the more apt I am to create a financial flow.

Well said, Valerie!

Does the Law of Attraction guarantee a smooth ride without bumps or detours? What about the challenges and unexpected events that seem to get in the way of getting what we want in our lives and in our businesses? The more we understand how the Law of Attraction works, the more we're able to turn those obstacles into opportunities.

It's important to remember that the script is the single most powerful tool you can use in attracting exactly what you want. Every detail matters. It sends such a clear and powerful message into the atmosphere that you'll want to carefully use words that describe what feels good to you.

> *Without leaps of imagination, or dreaming,*
> *we lose the excitement of possibilities.*
> *Dreaming, after all, is a form of planning.*
> —Gloria Steinem, author and journalist

Summary

Scripts are different from business plans in that they arise from our imagination and produce a total body, mind, and soul experience. Once the script is written, your plan is on autopilot. You can write a script for any event or topic. Every detail matters, however. Choose your words carefully and describe what feels good for you.

1 Stuart Litchman, *How to Get Lots of Money for Anything Fast!* (Santa Barbara, Calif.: Successful Ventures Publishing, Inc., 2004) (Originally published electronically as *How to Get Money Fast.*)

**As soon as we
have clarity, our
desire is on its way.**

Chapter 7

Contrast and Resistance: Change and Growth Motivators

Every person on Earth has a set of preferences as unique as their fingerprints; no one else has the exact same set. My preferences are right for me and yours are just right for you.

I prefer to be my own boss. I prefer to set my own schedule every day of the week. I prefer to work with people who are decisive and respond quickly. How did I discover my preferences? Through experiencing *contrast*—external events that didn't feel good—I gained the opportunity to become clear about what I love to do and how I love to do it.

What do I mean by *contrast*? If you smell something that doesn't smell good to you, that's contrast. If something costs more than you thought it would, that's contrast. If someone treats you rudely, that's contrast. Anything that doesn't feel good produces contrast.

Contrast is a prompt that something is unfinished, unexamined, or out of balance. It's a neutral term for your experience of external events that awaken your desire for change.

Contrast is essential.

Without contrast, we would remain clueless about ourselves and not make decisions.

Through experiencing contrast, I have discovered that working with indecisive people is a drain on my energy. Feeling tired, worn down, even exhausted is in contrast to the feelings I experience when I work with people who easily make a decision and stick with it. Decisive people energized me. As long as I ignored the contrast, I continued to attract clients who drained me. Finally, I'd experienced enough contrast to make a decision: *I want to work with people who are decisive.* Without the contrast, I would not have been able to make this decision and would still be attracting less-than-ideal clients.

However, I noticed that once in a while I still attracted the odd client who was indecisive. I asked my Inner Being how to stop that from happening. The answer came while I was teaching a TeleClass. I told my class, "I work *only* with people who are decisive." The shift was immediately apparent to me. Now I teach my students and clients to use the word "only" when they've truly had enough contrast.

Resistance slows the flow.

So why doesn't it just happen? Why does it take so long? What can we do to make it happen faster? Why do we continue to experience stuff we don't like?

If we could relax, joyfully expect our desires to be fulfilled, and enjoy life as it unfolds, all our desires would be manifested in seemingly record time. But most of us have beliefs and feelings operating inside us that resist the wonderful desires of our heart.

What you resist
will persist.

Resistance slows the flow of receiving goodness and well-being. Resistance is created when we:

- Feel negative emotions such as fear or anger, bitterness, or resentment.
- Don't allow ourselves to believe we're worthy of our desires.
- Try to speed up or force our way, rather than allowing the Law of Attraction to orchestrate and unfold all the events that need to take place so we can receive.

Resistance is the negative result of misguided beliefs, doubt, and unrecognized fear. It creates an internal contradictory vibration that can slow down and even cancel out the wonderful high-frequency vibrations we launched with our script.

When we say one thing but believe something else, we're sending mixed vibrations. The Law of Attraction responds to this mixture of vibrations. It doesn't sift through them, sorting them into piles for us: she really wants this; she doesn't want that; she changed her mind on this one. No, the Law of Attraction simply reads our vibrational meter and sends us more of the same.

We humans are so good at denying our feelings and burying them under false smiles, masks, and pat answers that we convince ourselves we're *just fine* when we're not. The Law of Attraction knows that the dominant desire of our Inner Being is to live a joy-filled, satisfying life that's free of guilt and deceit, so it mirrors that which is within—the good, the bad, and the ugly. With this *reality check*, we can acknowledge the belief, doubt, or fear that caused the negative vibration, examine it *briefly,* and decide if we want to keep it or change it.

As we begin to understand how the Law of Attraction works, we find we can no longer blame our parents, spouse, boss, or the unseen (God) for what occurs in our lives and businesses. Our own vibration creates every good or not-so-good event or situation. If we don't like what's showing up, then we can change our vibration so something better can arrive.

I experienced a very powerful demonstration of this truth during the formative days of TeleClass International. My task was to get money refunded on a software program that wasn't performing. I was frustrated with the vendor, since he had my credit card number and had charged additional money for installing the software, even though it didn't work properly. Plus, he had a no-refund policy. When the credit card company told me it couldn't remove the charge, I was frustrated and very angry!

It was the end of the workweek, and I left the city to relax at the nearby mineral springs. The drive gave me a little time to breathe out my anger and let go of most of my bad feelings.

I enjoyed myself at the mineral springs until a man disrupted my blissful repose by trying to start up a conversation in the pool. Every other word this man spoke was profane, aggressive, and loud. He even grabbed my inflatable pillow and tossed it about the pool. I couldn't wait to be rid of him.

When I escaped to my room, I asked myself what I had done to attract such a vile man. All of a sudden I understood—he was a direct reflection of the anger I'd been feeling right before I left home.

I decided then and there to give up my right to be angry about injustice and change my vibration.

There's only one sure way to change a negative feeling and that is to find a thought that feels better. I used the Law of Attraction T-Tool™ and asked myself this question: "So, if I don't want to feel ripped-off about the software, what do I want?"

I wrote: "I want to feel confident that I'll get my money back. It would feel good to know that my money is being fully refunded."

As my vibration started to rise, I realized that I was angry with myself because I thought I'd made a mistake. The Law of Attraction, however, teaches me that I never get it wrong; I just get to do it differently.

So, if I didn't do anything wrong, why was I so upset with myself? I wanted to impress my new business partner but making a poor choice of software and losing several hundred dollars in the process didn't look good. In that moment, I decided to let my pride go and tell my partner the truth. His response was, "It's a small amount of money when you consider how much we'll be making a year from now." Michael put the whole event into a new perspective.

By the way, I did receive the refund. All the money was reimbursed by check; there was no reversal on my credit card.

You'll attract the likeness of what you're vibrating.

The Law of Attraction was willing to give me what I wanted. My job was to let go of how it would come.

What about unrecognized resistance?

I've experienced other business events that seemed dramatic to me because of my *unrecognized resistance*. Being audited by Revenue Canada (the equivalent of the IRS in the U.S.) was such an event. I became so anxious upon receiving an unexpected letter from Revenue Canada that I knew the Law of Attraction was reflecting something I'd been resisting—organizing my financial records. The letter informed me that I was being audited for the year that Michael and I started our business. That same year I'd moved 1,800 miles from Saskatoon, Saskatchewan, to Victoria, British Columbia, and my dad had done our bookkeeping from his office in Texas. My financial records were spread across two countries.

"Why did this happen to me?" I lamented. "I couldn't have attracted *this* into my life, could I?"

But I had. I'd been ignoring the disarray of my records, possessed an unrecognized fear of government agencies, and had played the "poor dumb woman who doesn't know much about money" role all my adult life. So even though I understood the Law of Attraction and was leveraging it to create a life and business I loved, I had a number of fears and false beliefs creating resistance and conflicting vibrations.

Thank goodness for my business partner. Michael stayed calm and helped me find and organize all the paperwork. Each time he came over to help, I could feel my vibration rising.

Gradually, we found everything of importance and were able to reconstruct the tax information.

We even found a receipt for a $4,500 expense that our bookkeeper had missed. Suddenly, we were going to receive money *back* from the government. My vibration shot up like a rocket as our meeting with Revenue Canada approached.

About a week before we took the documentation into Revenue Canada, Michael said: "I'm picturing our revenue officer as a sensitive, caring person who is interested in learning about our company and understanding where we're coming from. I'm picturing our time in Revenue Canada's office as short, easy, and very positive."

That's exactly how it went. Michael's little script played out to the letter. About a month later, I received the good news that we could pick up our documentation and that our refund check was in the mail.

From that point on, we instructed our new bookkeeping team to sort all our documents in file folders according to Revenue Canada's reporting system. Now, if we ever need to, we can calmly pick up the files and take them straight to the auditor.

I have absolutely no fear of audits now. I know exactly where every receipt is. I know that our bookkeeping is organized, up to date, and accurate down to the penny. Believe me, this kind of clean feeling opens you up to receive more.

While most of the day-to-day causes of resistance are less dramatic than the examples provided, they can still cause long and unnecessary delays in delivering your heart's desires.

Is there any way to speed things up? Yes. In the next chapter, I'll tell you about a simple habit that will do just that and guarantee your success.

> *There are two primary choices in life:*
> *to accept conditions as they exist, or accept*
> *the responsibility for changing them.*
>
> —Denis Waitley, author of *The Psychology of Winning*

Summary

Contrast is a neutral term for the experience of external events that awaken our desire for change. Anything that doesn't feel good produces contrast. Contrast is essential—without it we wouldn't make decisions.

Resistance slows the flow of receiving goodness and well-being. It creates an internal contradictory vibration that can slow or even cancel the wonderful high-frequency vibrations we launched with our script.

Celebration,
appreciation,
gratitude, and
love all vibrate
at the
highest frequency.

Chapter 8

A Guarantee for Success

Here's a guarantee for success that is irrefutable: Celebrate each step of the way. Celebrate every achievement, every dollar that comes in, each tiny or huge manifestation that occurs as you grow your business, and you'll be successful. It's guaranteed.

The most common reason why we don't feel successful is because we take notice of and complain about how far we are from attaining our goal. Then we set our desire on reaching a specific goal within a certain time frame. As time goes by and our goal hasn't been fully realized, we start to doubt it will ever happen. We complain and say things like: "The Law of Attraction doesn't work" or "This doesn't work for me." This type of noticing keeps us stuck in the cycle of not accomplishing our goals or realizing our desires.

In traditional goal-setting, we usually celebrate only once, when the goal has been reached.

Picture the typical thermometer that any charitable agency uses to signify how far they are from achieving their campaign goal. Until the goal is reached, you'll notice that the main message evokes the fear of failure. This is intended to motivate us to give more generously. What really happens is that the media bombards us with messages like: "We haven't made it yet. We can't make it happen without you. We might not make it this time. Don't let this happen."

Yes, goals can be reached through sheer determination, hard work, and even with some bullying, guilt, and fear of failure. But the Law of Attraction offers an easier, softer way to experience success that is based on pure, positive energy pouring through our thoughts and actions.

Celebrate each step along the way: Karen's story.

Karen Krueger, the woman with the horse-healing business, offers a wonderful example of how celebrating every step of the way brings more opportunity to shape and craft a money-making business we love. Karen had developed the habit of celebrating each chance she had to meet her neighboring ranchers and be around their horses. Her goal was to increase her business of applying energetic treatments and natural remedies to other horses, the way she did to her own. And no matter how an opportunity presented itself, she celebrated each step that brought her closer to her goal. Here's more of Karen's story:

Recently I helped a friend with a broken arm do some of her horse blanket repair. It has always interested me, but I didn't know what it entailed. My mother used to sew all my clothes until I went to junior high school. There I learned to make my own clothes, which I continue to do to this day. Recently, I also began quilting.

Sewing has been integrated throughout my life. I have made clothes, leg wraps, and ankle boots for my horses. But I never knew how to earn money by sewing. At one time, I thought about selling my quilts, but people don't want to pay what they're worth.

I enjoyed helping my friend so much that I started my own horse blanket repair business. I love it. My husband was 100 percent supportive and provided the finances. I bought a used industrial sewing machine and my out-of-work neighbor built two beautiful worktables for me. Since we live so far out of town and there are lots of horses and farms, there will be plenty of work. I am visualizing that I am attracting the perfect clients who will come to me for their horse blanket repairs.

The amazing thing is that this is all falling together so perfectly. Both the materials and the equipment are coming to me easily. I just said to myself a few days ago that it would be so nice to find someone who is getting rid of old used blankets for me to practice on. Lo and behold, I was driving down the road the very next day and our neighbor had a bunch of junk by the road for the garbage pick-up. There was a pile of used horse blankets lying there. Well, I did a quick U-turn and drove up to the house to ask if I could rummage through their stuff and take the blankets. They told me to help myself; the blankets were really torn up and useless. Oh my gosh, there were seven perfectly salvageable blankets.

You know, Rebecca, I kept thinking of you and how you started with your website business that paved the way for your other businesses. I kept trying to think of something that would tie into the horse business that I would enjoy doing and could make money. I have always been independent, and this will give me my own income to support my other interests like attending horse-healing seminars.

I just finished one of the blankets tonight. I am sure this business will pave the way for me to get to know the people with whom

I am supposed to come in contact and, in turn, build rapport for my horse-healing business.

Three months later Karen wrote:

My horse blanket repair business is doing awesome. I have 10 upscale show barns that I am servicing on a weekly basis. After three months of being in business, I am averaging between $1,500 and $2,000 a month and there are more barns to service. I attract a new barn every other week.

I need to gauge how much I am able to handle. I remember your story, Rebecca, about how you attracted too many clients and how some of those clients were not fun to work with. So when I used my Law of Attraction T-Tool™, I wrote: "I don't want ... to feel swamped working with clients I don't enjoy. I do want ... happy clients with happy horses. I do want ... clients who are happy to pay me for my services. I do want ... to feel like I can easily service all my clients."

*One of the barns I work with is on Happy Canyon Road. While driving there one day, I thought about happiness, how important it was, and decided that I wanted to work **only** with barns that were happy and wanted my services. I know immediately if a place has an atmosphere I want to be in. I know I won't be going back to one of the barns I visited recently, because of the way they treat the horses. Not surprisingly, they don't want my services.*

So now, my horse-healing business is starting to develop. I am just thrilled. This is huge.

Karen's story is a perfect example of how one woman's celebration along the way has led to the fulfillment of her heart's desire.

Celebrate the closeness of the match!

While it's easy to celebrate all the good that is coming to you, I've found ways to celebrate situations that are not quite perfect. I remember a time when we were in negotiations with a corporation to train its staff. We worked hard to bring the corporation to the point of signing the contract, but at the last minute it pulled out. Instead of moaning about not getting the contract, I decided to celebrate how close we came with a response of, "Wow. That was a close match." I call this: "Celebrating the closeness of the match."

When something shows up that isn't 100 percent what I want, I notice the parts of it that *are* a match. Then I *briefly* observe what isn't complementary and ask myself, "So, if I don't want this, what do I want?" I use those pieces that aren't a perfect fit to get more clarity.

Yes, it takes effort to deliberately search for something positive to celebrate. It seems easier or more natural to notice what is negative. Both choices come with differing results. What results do you want in your life?

If you form the habit of celebrating each success along the way, you'll reach your goal—fully, completely, and beyond your wildest dreams.

The Law of Attraction Training Center was a success long before the first student enrolled. Success began years earlier with the first inkling I had of creating an over-the-telephone training course for people who want to learn about the Law of Attraction. From the time it was conceived until its birth,

I was honing the skills needed to launch a successful virtual training company. All my prior businesses contributed to the formation and success of the Law of Attraction Training Center:

1. As a Law of Attraction Coach, my clients taught me what was important to them. I developed Attraction Tools to aid them in gaining clarity, raising their vibrations, and receiving their desires. The curriculum for the Certified Law of Attraction Practitioner's Course already existed within me.

2. With skills I had refined as a web developer through Aurora Websites, I was able to quickly conceptualize the entire website, which is easy to navigate and user-friendly.

3. Through growing and developing TeleClass International, I was perfecting the catalog and registration system needed to automatically administer student registrations for the center.

4. Through our subsidiary company, Telephone Bridge Services, I acquired the technology to hold and record high-quality classes over the telephone.

5. For years I gave free TeleClasses, perfecting my skills as a TeleLeader so I could easily and confidently deliver information and guide students in experiencing the Law of Attraction.

6. I cultivated friendships with like-minded people. When the Training Center was ready, the faculty was already assembled.

Yes, I celebrated when the first student showed up and when the first graduate completed all the requirements for certification. It was natural to celebrate after so many successes.

How do you define success? How does it look and feel to you? How do you recognize success when it shows up?

I measure success by the amount of joy in my life. The more joy I experience in my businesses, the more successful I am as an entrepreneur. The more joy I experience in my business relationships, the faster and easier my businesses grow.

Money follows joy.

When I'm joyful, celebrating and appreciating all aspects of my life and business, the money appears. I find creative ways to expand, integrate, and streamline my businesses. As a result, my businesses flourish and prosper.

If you appreciate and joyfully celebrate each success along the way, your continued success is guaranteed.

Success isn't the key to happiness. Happiness is the key to success. If you love what you're doing, you'll be successful.

-—Albert Schweitzer, philosopher, physician and humanitarian
Winner of the 1952 Nobel Peace Prize

Summary

Your success is guaranteed when you celebrate every achievement, as well as each situation that isn't quite perfect. I call this "Celebrating the closeness of the match." Celebrate how close you've come to achieving your dream, rather than focusing on how far you have to go before you obtain it fully. The measure of success is joy.

Clear communication is the cornerstone upon which to build solid relationships.

Chapter 9

Working in Harmony

Something happens to your existing relationships when your vibration changes. Sometimes the change in you brings out the best in your partner or associates—and sometimes the friction that was held beneath the surface rises to the top and begs to be addressed. Either way, when your vibration changes, you create an opportunity to learn more about the people you work with and to develop new "people skills."

Throughout this book, I've shared some glimpses into the unique partnership that Michael Losier and I experience in owning TeleClass International. We have been practicing and perfecting the art of co-creating a virtual business (our offices are in separate locations) using the Law of Attraction for more than five years. In this chapter, I'll share with you some of our secrets to working together harmoniously. You will learn how Michael and I learned to communicate in ways we each can easily relate to. I'll share with you some of the core values we agree on, and I'll answer some common questions about how to keep your vibration high while working in a not-quite-perfect workplace.

Communication is at the heart of every good relationship.

Very early in our relationship, Michael asked me to complete a little questionnaire to determine my dominant communication style. From his NLP (Neuro Linguistic Programming) background, he knew how important it is, when it comes to maintaining a high vibration, to deliver a message using words other people can relate to easily. The basis of NLP is the four communication styles:

- Visual
- Auditory
- Kinesthetic
- Auditory-Digital

Each person processes information predominately in one style. While the other styles are available to us, we may not find them as easily accessible. Michael already knew that his style was primarily visual (which meant he needed to see the "big picture" first) and suspected I was auditory-digital (which meant I processed information very quickly, in a sequential and step-by-step manner).

When working with Michael, I discovered that he tuned me out when I used too many words or was explaining a technical process. Once I understood that his communication style was primarily visual, I quickly realized the best way to convey detailed information to Michael was to literally draw pictures. I used my computer graphics program to diagram complicated processes such as websites and flow charts.

I also used visual words such as look, see, picture, and focus. And to elicit quick responses, I asked questions using key visual words like: "How does that look to you?" "How do you picture it?" "Can you see if this works for you?"

He, in turn, appealed to my auditory-digital communication style by using words like think, process, or figure out and asked questions that included key words that appealed to my thought process: "What do you think about that?" and "I know you can figure this out."

We learned that when the other person feels stressed, they retreat into certain moods or mindsets: I tend toward paranoia and resentfulness, while Michael becomes rigid and inflexible.

We discovered that we can do certain things to help ourselves (or suggest them to each other). If I'm feeling stressed about something, I usually need more information. Satisfying my *need to know* goes a long way in reducing tension. I find that spending time alone and uninterrupted recharges my battery.

Michael's way to reduce stress is to diagram or make lists on his whiteboard. If he's feeling overwhelmed about a project, just writing out all the steps necessary will bring him relief. For me, it's enough to know the logical sequence of the project and hold that information in my mind.

Michael gets energized by being with people—especially when he's in the spotlight. I get rejuvenated by being alone and focused on a project.

Communication is at the heart of our good relationship. It's also the foundation of TeleClass International's Certified TeleLeader Training program. It's so valuable that I obtained permission from Linda Storey, a Certified NLP Counselor, to provide you with her "Understanding the Four Communication Styles," which includes the important characteristics of each style, a questionnaire, and a score sheet. You'll find these in Appendix B of this book. By filling out the questionnaire, you'll learn enough about the four communications styles to identify other people's predominant style just by listening to the words they use in normal, everyday conversations.

The more you learn about your business partner, associates, or colleagues, the easier it will be to keep your vibration high. When you both (or all) vibrate at a high level, everything you need to know, say, or do will come to you more easily. Your business can thrive!

The agenda is a vital communication tool in business.

How could something as simple as an *agenda* become vital (necessary to sustain life) to a company? Yet the agenda has been the mainstay of our company and our sanity! In the beginning, Michael was working part-time at his government job in Victoria and I was working from my home in Saskatoon. I would get an idea or think of something that would be important to TeleClass International, but I had to wait until Michael was home from his day job to share that great idea. I found it frustrating to have to wait—not knowing for sure when Michael would be available. Often he needed more time to process my ideas and felt pressured to agree with me right when the new idea was expressed. We both felt some tension and uneasiness, until we discovered the agenda.

Here's how the agenda works: (Remember that we both work from our home offices and all our business meetings are held over the telephone. Headsets are mandatory!)

1. We decide on the best dates and times to have business meetings. Sometimes we schedule our meetings three months in advance. Usually we hold two meetings a week, for two hours at a time. When TeleClass International was in the developmental stage, we'd book additional meetings.

2. As soon as one meeting is finished, we start building the agenda for the next meeting. We do this by email, with something like: "Agenda for May 10th" in the subject line.

3. We're both responsible for adding items of importance to the agenda.

4. We both get to see what's on the other person's mind before the meeting time. If needed, we ask for clarification or more details to be added to the agenda.

5. At the time of our business meeting, we both print out the agenda.

6. We always start our business meetings sharing our Law of Attraction success stories. It sets the tone for the rest of the meeting and starts us out on a high vibration. It's a great way to celebrate successes along the way and to encourage each other.

7. Next, we prioritize the agenda. We discuss which items need to be dealt with first and which ones can wait.

8. Then we plunge in! Our goal is to clear the agenda in two hours—sometimes we've had up to 20 items to work through. Since the less important items are managed last, if we don't get to them, they are first on the next agenda.

9. We use the Law of Attraction T-Tool™ to get clarity on any subject:

   a. Ideal clients

   b. Networking meetings

   c. Referrals

   d. Sales

   e. Publicity

   f. Associates

Working over the phone this way, in focused blocks of time, allows us to accomplish in two hours what normally takes six to eight hours to do.

You can introduce the idea of the agenda to people you work with anytime there is a meeting coming up—co-workers, supervisors, business owners all benefit from having an agenda they have contributed to.

Core values help make relationships harmonious.

Some of my biggest sensations of "contrast" have come when I tried to partner with people who did not hold similar core values.

A sage once wrote: "How can two walk together, unless they agree?" As we attract to ourselves people who want to work with us and who seem to have skills that would be compatible, it's important to discover very early in the relationship whether there is agreement **on a heart level**. Some people have learned how to say what they think you want to hear. The Law of Attraction teaches me to tune in to what they are vibrating and notice if their words and their vibration match. When they don't match, I have a general sense of uneasiness or confusion. Sometimes I have the thought, "Something isn't quite right" or "Something doesn't line up here." When I notice how uncomfortable the discord of their words and vibrations makes me feel, I ask the Law of Attraction for clarity. Inevitably, the person will say or do something that demonstrates their true self.

I don't try to change other people. I just get a reading on their core values and decide if theirs are the same or close to mine. If not, I disengage from further contact with them. If their core values are compatible with mine, then I'll continue to develop and nurture a healthy relationship with them.

Do you know what your core values are? Here are some of the core values Michael and I share and why they are important to us and our business relationship and, therefore, to our business success.

Honesty: Nothing builds trust in a relationship like honesty. Honesty includes:

- Being aware of yourself and how you feel about each aspect of your business.

- Having the skills to communicate your feelings without judgment or making the other person "wrong."

- Letting someone know when your focus or energy needs to shift from the business to something personal.

- Not withholding information the other person needs to know to make an informed decision.

- Asking for what you want, instead of complaining about what you don't like. We quickly learned to use the Law of Attraction T-Tool™ to ask for what we want. If one of us forgets and starts complaining, we give that person a "30-second BMW" (30 seconds to Bitch, Moan, and Whine) then ask, "So what *do* you want?"

"So what *do* you want?" That question alone is powerful enough to shift the atmosphere in any workplace to positive, good-feeling, high-frequency vibrations. Write that question down. Put it in a conspicuous place in your work area. I wrote it on a neon-colored three-by-five-inch card so I would remember to ask: "So what *do* you want?"

Equality: Equality has been an important core value for me. Yet, for most of my life I found myself in situations where being female was seen as inferior to being male. The community in which I grew up seemed to feel threatened by my intelligence, how quickly I processed information, and how easily I assumed leadership roles. In a male-dominated community, these qualities were detrimental for a woman. Needless to say, I was always pushing against the norms of my community.

As an adult, I have met people who value the contributions of men and women. Working with these people as their equals feels wonderful!

Equality is about sharing the responsibilities, the workload, and the rewards. Michael and I both know how to ask for a review if the responsibilities are getting a bit lopsided.

Financial responsibility: Michael and I share a desire to be "squeaky clean" when it comes to finances. Between the two of us, we share three bookkeepers and an accountant to keep track of all our businesses—down to the penny.

We gladly pay for their expertise because we're both committed to financial transparency. We know that financial irresponsibility causes resistance and financial cleanliness allows us to attract *more* money faster.

We only do what we enjoy: You might not consider this a core value, but it's at the core of our successful business partnership. In the beginning, we did everything ourselves—from creating the websites, to teaching all the TeleLeader Trainings, to balancing the bank statements and bookkeeping. We made a decision to always know every aspect of our business by doing it first, before we hand a part over to someone else. So, in the beginning, we tracked every credit card transaction and posted every expense on our spreadsheet. Then when neither of us wanted to do that job, we handed it over to others and taught them what to do. When Michael's speaking engagements took him away from Victoria, we trained someone else to deliver the TeleLeader Training. When various administrative tasks became laborious, we hired an administrative assistant. The rule is: "We do only what we love and enjoy." If a task becomes less than joyful, we turn it over to someone who finds it a pleasure to do.

A desire for each other's success: I would call this a core value because this deep desire for the other person's success and welfare is what keeps our business relationship harmonious even while it changes. As we have each developed other interests and the focus of our lives has shifted, we have been able to redefine our business partnership. Through mutual respect and expressions of appreciation, we share in the other's success outside the parameters of our business partnership.

His success is my bliss. My success is Michael's happiness. And the measure of success is joy.

Do you have a clear understanding, picture, or idea about your core values? Write down the words that best describe those characteristics you value the most. Ask your Inner Being to bring to mind times when you unknowingly did something or made a decision contrary to a core value. How did you feel? What made you feel better?

Several years ago, Michael and I were about to go into partnership with a fellow who had a great skill for marketing. After spending a few days with him in person, we then worked with him over the phone. After about a month, I noticed I was feeling very frustrated and blocked whenever I had to deal with him. Finally I was able to put my finger on the problem—he didn't see me as equal to Michael because I'm a woman. When I shared this with Michael, he agreed that equality was not this man's reality. Michael had sensed something wasn't a match from the first time we'd met him. Together, we politely told the gentleman we would not continue doing business with him.

We must honor ourselves and those values we hold as true if we want to run a successful business.

Start your core values list today and notice what happens when you honor them and when you don't.

Five common questions:

Often people will write and ask questions about the Law of Attraction as it pertains to their businesses. Here are the five most common questions about how to keep your vibration high while working in a not-quite-perfect workplace:

1. How can I get my co-workers to become more positive?

While you can't force people to be positive, you can create a cheerful atmosphere in which they may find it easier to be upbeat. Ask yourself how it feels when others think poorly of you. Then imagine how it feels when your friends or colleagues think you are wonderful. Which thought feels better? And when we choose to focus on the positive aspects in others, we allow them to respond in the most positive ways. When we choose to only focus on the positive aspects in others, we keep our own vibration high.

Many years ago, my father, Tom Utley, was hired as the financial comptroller of a medium-size manufacturing company in Burbank, California. It didn't take long to realize the accounting department was in serious trouble. Morale was low. Employees were dissatisfied, unhappy, and bickering with one another. If anyone made a mistake, failed to meet a deadline, or did not follow through on an assignment, negative comments were passed around. Employees were often embarrassed by these events.

My dad asked himself, "How can I approach this problem without further damaging morale, and without adding to the problem with negative criticism of what I see?" Intuitively he decided to take a positive approach.

Every time an employee met a deadline, completed a journal entry correctly, balanced an account, or made a worthy suggestion, Tom complimented that employee in the presence of others. Even when performing his own duties correctly, Tom openly praised himself for doing "good work." Not once did he make a negative comment about anyone or anything that occurred in the accounting department.

About four to six weeks later, it was obvious that the snide jabs and critical comments that had characterized the department no longer existed. Instead, employees openly celebrated their own efforts and complimented others on theirs.

2. I want out of my present job so badly. How can I speed things up so I can quit?

The best way to shorten the time spent in a negative situation is to focus on all the positives you can. If you can't find a single positive aspect of your present job, just act as if you *are* working in a fun place. The Law of Attraction doesn't know the difference between remembering the past, observing the present or imagining the future. So if you act as if you like your job, you'll either attract a different set of situations in that job or you'll soon find yourself working in a new place that feels great!

Remember, your thoughts and feelings today are creating your tomorrow. So, if you keep noticing what you don't like about your current job, you'll attract another job with a similar set of challenges.

3. Will there ever be a time when I attract only good or wonderful things into my world?

No. We need the contrast of "not-so-wonderful" experiences to bring us to the point of making a decision. Without contrast, we become passive. Any contrast we experience can be used to derive more clarity about what would feel better, thus creating more experiences that feel good.

4. Is it possible to attract a specific person, project, job or business into my life?

It's possible to focus so intently we force events that bring us together with specific people. However, it may not be an enjoyable experience. If the other party wasn't looking for you or your business, the experience may feel like an intrusion or manipulation to them. It's better to become clear about the essence of your desire and let the Law of Attraction bring to you people, projects, or business that are a closer match to your vibration.

5. Is it possible to attract something I didn't ask for (e.g., a business setback)?

You may not have consciously "asked for" something. However, the Law of Attraction is responding to some forgotten, ignored, or subconscious vibration. And this is one way to get you to pay attention to that vibration.

Once you acknowledge the operation of a vibration of fear, doubt, or disbelief, you can decide to change that vibration into one of trust, belief, or affirmative action. All it takes is a decision to choose a thought that feels better.

Even if you are currently in a perfect business or work experience, you can make it better. The Law of Attraction teaches us that we get more of what we place our focus and attention on. You do have the power, and now the tools, to create a business, job, or career you *love*!

> *Dreams come true. Without that possibility,*
> *nature would not incite us to have them.*
>
> —John Updike, American author

Summary

Communication is as vital to a good business relationship as it is to a good marriage. In both instances, understanding your partner's dominant communication style means using words they can more easily relate to. Another important tool is working with an agenda in business meetings so there is always a pre-arranged forum for discussion (perhaps marriage partners should consider using an agenda as well). The most important consideration, however, is choosing a business partner who shares your core values. We must honor ourselves and those values we hold as true if we want to be successful in business.

The Law of Attraction doesn't know the difference between remembering the past, observing the present, or imagining the future.

Chapter 10

Putting It All Together

We've come to this place in our lives because we're ready to learn an easier, softer, and gentler way of living. The Law of Attraction teaches us that we become a magnet for whatever we put our focus and attention on, regardless of whether it's positive or negative.

We have a marvelous meter within us that tells us when something is good for us or when it isn't. That meter is our feelings and emotions. When something feels good, it's good for us. When something doesn't feel good, it isn't good for us. We don't need to understand why; we just need to notice the way everything feels and choose what feels good and right for us.

We're powerful magnets. We draw to ourselves people, opportunities, situations, or events that match the vibrations we emit through our thoughts, feelings, emotions, or moods.

The more choices we make in favor of what feels good to us, the more we're aligned with our purpose in life. That's how we become powerful, deliberate magnets.

The Law of Attraction Formula teaches us how to be more deliberate in the type of vibrations we offer.

Formula for Desired Experience:
A + B + C = DE (Desired Experience)

Step A: Get Clarity

The Law of Attraction allows us to experience situations of discomfort and contrast, as well as joy, so that we can achieve clarity about ourselves. Based on what feels good and right to us, we begin to get a clear picture of our purpose in life and how to meet that purpose. This picture translates into a desire to create a business, find a job, or have a career that is in alignment with our purpose or true self.

We can use the Law of Attraction T-Tool™ to get clarity around *every* aspect of our life and business.

Step B: Raise Our Vibration

As we make more choices that are in alignment with our true selves, we experience more joy and emit higher vibrations, thus creating an even more positive atmosphere in which to realize all our heart's desires and secret dreams.

These three phrases can be used to deliberately raise our vibrational frequency around our desired outcome:

"I'm in the process of attracting my ideal …"

"The Law of Attraction is in the process of …"

"I love it when …"

Step C: Allow What We've Asked for to Arrive

To receive the desired outcome, we must *allow* it into our lives. We need to replace dark, cloudy thoughts of doubt and self-sabotage with open, clear thoughts of joyful anticipation. The degree to which we are certain of our desire is an indicator of the degree to which we are *allowing* all the goodness of life to flow to and through us.

DE = Desired Experience

To actually experience all our desires in our career, celebrate each step along the way. As we look for evidence of our wishes being satisfied, our journey will be full of joy and we will feel content.

When we learn to embrace the obstacles along the way, they *can* be converted to gold. Each pocket of resistance or episode of contrast is an opportunity to learn more about ourselves. Ask yourself, "If I don't like this, what would I like?"

If we form the habit of celebrating each success along the way, we'll reach our goal fully, completely, and beyond our wildest dreams.

It's the law.

As we grow in knowing, accepting, and honoring ourselves, we become capable of knowing, accepting, and honoring others. We find that we're more tolerant of others, allowing them to grow and change at their own rate in ways that are best for them. When others express a desire to live a joyful and rewarding life, we'll be able to encourage and lift them up, while holding the light on their path.

This could happen to you ...

In the few short years I've known about the Law of Attraction, I've been renovating every aspect of my life—both personal and business-related.

I started out feeling trapped in a marriage that was unfulfilling, betrayed by a community that discriminated against my gender, exhausted from caring for children with challenging handicaps and aging, dying parents. Today I love the freedom of being myself. I'm excited about the resurgence of my gifts and talents, thrilled to be making and spending money the way I enjoy most, and relishing the best and healthiest relationships with my family and friends.

There's no doubt about it—going from no job in 30 years to owning seven businesses in five years has brought me deep satisfaction. There was a time, during my early 20s, when I felt I had "a good head for business." I thought I'd be able to work alongside my husband, and I was reading about office procedures while mentally organizing his soon-to-be office and getting a grasp on the business end of his medical practice. But that was not to be. I was not welcome to participate in his life this way. So I threw myself into raising a large family. I stayed at home and sought to find my life's fulfillment through raising children.

Well, I did a good job of raising my children. All five live independent, productive lives. My two oldest children are in helping professions—one is a paramedic, the other an interpreter for the deaf. My middle daughter is a part-time hair stylist—married and raising two young boys. My daughter who has Down's syndrome lives on her own with support and encouragement from her dad and me. And the youngest child lives in a wonderful group home, where many loving people can support him as he experiences life with Down's syndrome and autism.

If you can believe,
you can receive.

Now it's my turn to see what I can do for myself. Like many women in their 50s, I have fewer obligations to others, time to focus on my own health and spiritual/emotional growth. I can choose to be with people or to be entirely alone with myself. The journey of self-discovery and self-appreciation has been full of surprises and joy. I've discovered a wonderful person—me. And I am shameless about what I love and enjoy doing. I love life! I attribute this turnaround to that wonderful decision to let go of the old framework and embrace the new one—the Law of Attraction.

We've often heard the Joseph Campbell saying: "Follow your bliss." Well, for me, following my bliss has been like following a trail of bread crumbs. The first crumb was the resurrection of the creative part of me—that part that loves color, shape, form, and function. The next crumb was when I acknowledged how important communication is to me—it's like breathing. If you're not breathing, you're not alive. Relationships need lots of good, wholesome, healthy communication or they are not relationships at all. The next crumb to come to my attention was the Internet where I could indulge in all the creativity and communication I wanted. I feel like a chocoholic in a candy store! Building websites satisfies my craving to constantly create with "color, shape, form, and function." Need I say more?

I've had a full-grown teacher in me since I was seven years old. Now the teacher gets to teach to her heart's content through the technology of teleconference bridges. My audience is not limited to a few people in my locale; my audience on the teleconference bridge is global!

The writer in me has gone underground in the past—but she flourishes again as I bring this book to a close.

For the longest time, I felt as though I'd wasted 30 years of my life. I'd missed so many opportunities for self-fulfillment—I thought I'd never catch up. However, recently I had the most amazing realization: "I'm caught up now." I am exactly today where I would be if I'd taken a different road. Nothing was lost. All my hopes, all my dreams, all my desires, and all I'd imagined have come true.

Now I'm dreaming new dreams ... bigger, broader, deeper, and wider dreams. I'll need more than another 50 years to live them!

> *Do what your heart tells you,*
> *not what the world sells you.*
> *If you can dream it, you can do it.*
>
> —Walt Elias Disney, founder Walt Disney Company

Appendix A:

Elevations® Skills Assessment

Visit www.lawofattractionresources.com to download a printable copy of the Elevations® Skills Assessment.

The first step in creating a business or attracting a job you love is to gain clarity about what you love to do. This adaptation of the Elevations® Skills Assessment[1] is a tool that can help you identify which business skills you enjoy most, which skills you dislike (these attribute to burnout), and which skills you would like to develop.

Instructions

Fold a sheet of paper into three equal columns.

Starting with the column on the left, label the columns Highest, Moderate, and Lowest.

Ask someone to read the skills list to you while you place each skill in the column that best describes how motivated you are to use it. Trust your gut feeling. Focus on the feeling of using the skill even if you still need to develop those talents. If certain ones appeal to you but you feel you have no experience with them, circle them. You can come back to them later and decide if you want to develop those skills.

Elevations® Skills List

These skills are grouped under four different skill types, which are explained in detail starting on page 146.

A. ORGANIZER

<u>Coordinate Events</u>: Plan and organize event details like times, facilities, and agendas.

<u>Audit</u>: Examine records or accounts for accuracy.

<u>Remember Details</u>: Memorize and recall particulars.

<u>Implement Procedures</u>: Carry out or put into effect procedures or protocols.

<u>Appraise</u>: Evaluate the value of something.

<u>Categorize</u>: Classify or arrange into categories.

<u>Organize Projects</u>: Plan, arrange, or systematize tasks to meet specified goals.

<u>Calculate/Compute</u>: Count or figure amounts.

<u>Use Space Efficiently</u>: Arrange physical elements for greatest utility or ease of movement.

<u>Retain Facts</u>: Hold and maintain knowledge of demonstrable truths.

<u>Monitor Quality</u>: Oversee process to ensure standards are met.

<u>Control Inventory</u>: Purchase and track supplies, goods, or merchandise.

<u>Budget</u>: Plan for expenditures or allocation of resources.

<u>Map Routes</u>: Plan and delineate paths or courses of travel or transportation.

<u>Estimate Costs</u>: Make approximate calculations or preliminary assessments of costs.

<u>Edit Reports/Stories</u>: Prepare reports or stories for presentation or publication.

B. LIBERATOR

<u>Add Humor and Fun</u>: Contribute a funny or amusing element to environment or process.

<u>Troubleshoot</u>: Identify sources of trouble or causes of malfunction.

<u>Negotiate</u>: Use persuasive skills to come to terms or reach agreement.

<u>Utilize Technology</u>: Solve problems with computer software, mechanical devices, or electronics.

<u>Make Crafts</u>: Create artistic objects with one's hands.

<u>Draft</u>: Create a visual representation of a plan for construction or manufacture.

<u>Improvise</u>: Create spontaneously or make do with available resources.

<u>Risk</u>: Undertake high-risk projects or tasks to increase profits or save lives.

<u>Market Products/Services</u>: Identify target consumers and develop strategies to sell products/services to them.

<u>Paint</u>: Apply coating or pigments for artistic expression or utility.

<u>Use Tools</u>: Employ or manipulate hand-held implements.

Repair: Fix or restore to working condition after damage.

Design Landscapes: Conceptualize planting arrangements to meet functional and decorative goals.

Prepare Food: Assemble ingredients and create appealing meals.

Mobilize: Rally, prepare, and coordinate others, especially in response to crisis.

Use Physical Dexterity: Demonstrate skill and coordination in use of body.

C. FACILITATOR

Teach/Instruct: Impart knowledge or skill through presentation, example, or experience.

Interview: Direct questions or conversation to elicit facts, viewpoints, or statements.

Speak in Public: Address groups of people in a public setting.

Design Interiors: Conceptualize arrangement and decoration of work or living spaces.

Motivate Others: Provide incentive and generate excitement to achieve goals.

Heal: Restore to health or soundness, cure.

Serve Customers: Assess needs and provide appropriate goods and services.

Inspire: Arouse emotions and stimulate to creativity or action.

Listen: Tune in or pay attention in an effort to hear and understand.

<u>Collaborate</u>: Work together with others in a joint effort.

<u>Counsel</u>: Exchange opinions and ideas and/or give guidance.

<u>Entertain Guests</u>: Extend hospitality toward visitors.

<u>Conduct Therapy</u>: Attend to emotional needs. Provide treatment for illness or disability.

<u>Lead Teams</u>: Guide or direct work of organized groups.

<u>Coach</u>: Provide encouragement, brainstorm ideas.

<u>Use Color</u>: Conceptualize the use of and apply pigment for creative expression.

D. INNOVATOR

<u>Design Systems</u>: Conceptualize methods or procedures for operations or processes.

<u>Demonstrate Confidence</u>: Exhibit belief in oneself and one's capabilities or expertise.

<u>Plan Long-range</u>: Formulate a scheme or program to achieve long-term goals.

<u>Brainstorm</u>: Generate ideas and explore alternatives and other options.

<u>Coordinate Events</u>: Plan and organize event details such as times, facilities, and agendas.

<u>Explore New Concepts</u>: Express openness and inquire about new or unfamiliar ideas.

<u>Strategize</u>: Develop a comprehensive plan of action.

<u>Visualize/Forecast</u>: Form a mental image and anticipate events or conditions.

Analyze: Examine methodically and thoroughly.

Investigate: Make detailed inquiry to examine cause and effect.

Advise: Use knowledge and expertise to make suggestions or recommendations.

Research: Investigate or study using books, interviews, or the Internet.

Manage Projects: Oversee organization and execution of tasks to achieve goals.

Consult: Assess client needs and give expert advice as a professional.

Use Logic: Employ reasoning and rational thought processes.

Invent: Use imagination and ingenuity to conceptualize or create something new.

Invest Finances: Commit money or capital for profit gain.

Understanding the Elevations® Skills Assessment

Read over the skills you placed in each of the three columns, starting with the left-hand column, "Highest." Do those skills excite you? Do they raise your vibrations? These are your motivating skills.

The skills in the "Moderate" column could be ones you like but are tired of using, or haven't used much, and ones you want to develop more. Circle those skills you may wish to pursue.

The skills under "Lowest" are commonly ones you have no interest in or are *burnout* skills. If any of these skills are an integral part of your business, you may want to consider alternative ways to manage them. For example, if you wrote "budget" in this column, you may want to consider hiring someone else to do this for you.

Next are descriptive overviews for each of the four skill groups.

Elevations® Skills Assessment Description of Types

A. ORGANIZER:

Organizers enjoy careers that are stable, well-paid, and offer promotional opportunities. They seek clear direction and will follow through on their commitments. They are attracted to professional offices that provide the practical resources needed to do the job. They like to feel they are contributing to the financial success of an organization. They may be attracted to the trades, a wide range of administrative occupations, technology, or government services. They are responsible and will look for a boss or partner who appreciates their contributions .

B. LIBERATOR:

Liberators enjoy careers that are exciting, flexible, and fun. They may enjoy working outdoors or in jobs that allow freedom of mobility. Their interests can vary across many industries such as biotechnology, transportation, marketing, or agriculture. In addition, they may have a second job or home-based business that supplements their day job and keeps life interesting. Job satisfaction often comes from providing practical solutions to immediate problems. Short projects are often appealing. They look for a boss or partner who understands their need for independence and appreciates their ability to manage unpredictability with ease.

C. FACILITATOR:

Facilitators enjoy careers that are meaningful and helpful to others. They are often attracted to jobs that allow them to work in casual, natural environments. They will decorate their office space with live plants, pictures of loved ones, and colorful art to create a warm, inviting atmosphere. Careers in health care, education, social services, art, and international relations are appealing. They have strong interpersonal skills and seek a supportive, team-oriented work environment. They appreciate a boss or partner who provides clear feedback on a regular basis.

D. INNOVATOR:

Innovators enjoy careers that allow for creativity and problem solving. They enjoy working with state-of-the-art tools and resources. Frequently they look for better ways to operate systems or produce products. Learning and gaining knowledge is a major motivator. Industries that often interest an Innovator include science, technology, higher education, law, business management, and health care. They enjoy the initiation of a project or program but may lose interest once everything is running smoothly. They will look for an organization that responds to logical and well-researched perspectives.

Note: These skill types are very general. Keep in mind your unique blend of life experiences and your authentic self. This is just a tool to gather clues about what motivates you, what you love about your present career, and what you don't.

....

1 Adapted from *Elevations®, the Career Discovery Tool,* published by Scully Career Associates, Inc. Copyrighted and patent pending, 2004. To take the complete version of this career assessment, visit http://www.ElevateYourCareer.com.

Appendix B:

Understanding the Four Communication Styles

© Copyright 2004 Linda Storey

*Certified Master NLP Practitioner and
Certified NLP Counselor*

*Adapted from the writings of Linda Storey and used
with permission.*

Communication is at the heart of every good relationship.

Learning an effective way to communicate clearly is a sure way to raise your vibration both at work and at home.

All our experiences are a result of what we see, hear, feel, touch, and smell, and we use one of these senses as our primary way of processing information. In Neuro Linguistic Programming (NLP), these four ways of processing are referred to as the "four communication styles." They are:

- Visual
- Auditory
- Kinesthetic
- Auditory-Digital

Regardless of your type of business, having the ability to speak in all four communication styles will give you the flexibility needed to create rapport, and to maintain it.

As you've noticed, not everyone communicates the same way. Many people think, see, hear, and feel differently than you do. If your communication is clear with others, if understanding is easily achieved and you're getting along just fine, then don't do anything differently.

If, on the other hand, you find you're becoming frustrated or impatient, can't see the logic in what others are saying, and are generally experiencing your communication as stuck and unsatisfactory, then this is where having the flexibility and knowledge to speak another person's language really comes in handy.

Specifically and deliberately chosen words and phrases can help get things back on track. Understanding the behavior tendencies, as well as the words, of each of the four styles is also very useful. Here are a few general ideas for using this information to your best advantage.

Visual style:

A person who learns and processes information quickly and prefers things to move along at a fast and steady pace is most likely using the visual processing style. These people tend to enjoy shorter, 30-minute meetings rather than an hour because they are able to cover a lot of information in a short period of time. They enjoy the big picture and can get bored and impatient if bogged down with too many details. The visual processing style is fast and changing, allowing them to easily move from subject to subject at lightening speed and maintain high levels of energy.

Timing is important. Visual people love it when meetings start on time and end on time. They can appear rigid if not given enough time to change their picture, especially if a plan has been changed without their knowledge. Given enough notice, they are able to change their picture and become flexible. When choosing a team for a new project, visual style people excel at the beginning and planning stage. Get someone else to do the thorough details. Their strengths lie in their creativity and their ability to get things done.

Auditory style:

When you meet someone who absolutely loves to take an idea, theory, object, or concept and improve it, or you notice they're always inventing one thing or another from scratch, you're most likely in the presence of a person who processes from the auditory style. They are able to easily come up with creative new ideas, at times to the exhaustion of others, and until they choose one to deal with, they can become overwhelmed and scattered. Working with a coach or a support person to help them stay on track, taking the idea and prioritizing it step by step, and being accountable are ways of helping them bring fabulous ideas to completion.

They are gifted at entertaining others with their storytelling and joke telling. Words are important to them, especially how they are used and the tone involved. They have a tendency to get irritated if they don't feel heard, or if they are interrupted. To make sure they get their point across, they might repeat the story from the very beginning. They tend to be private individuals who share openly if trust has been established and if they know the information will be kept private if requested.

Kinesthetic style:

If you have a client who arrives for a session with a tote bag containing water, a journal for taking notes, a pair of socks, and a few snacks, then chances are he or she is kinesthetic. They are comfort seekers and make sure they have it wherever they go. In a training room, a kinesthetic person might use two chairs, one to sit on and one for the tote bag. They have a tendency to wiggle a lot until they get comfortable and then are able to remain still for long periods of time.

The kinesthetic style is supportive, nurturing, fun-loving, and cares a great deal for how other people feel. It's important to them that people get along and that projects run smoothly. They can, however, take on the feelings of others and become "emotional sponges." Learning how to detach and how to say no help the kinesthetic person stay grounded and balanced. As team players, they are great with details and make good decisions from the gut-feeling level once they have logically collected the data and information they need. It can seem as though they are "beyond words" at times and are working at a deeper level. It is often difficult for them to put their feelings into words. In an ideal world they prefer working on one project at a time. Too many choices tend to overwhelm, which can lead to procrastination. They respond well to people who give them the time they need to process and especially feel good when someone offers to give them a hand in completing a task.

Auditory-Digital style:

This style might be the most difficult one to detect if you are just paying attention to the words people use. These people tend to use words and phrases from all four styles. If that's the case, then pay attention to some of their behavior traits. For example, they might use their hands when letting you know they want to discuss three things with you. They enjoy having all their ducks in a row. Sequence and order give them a sense of personal control so, rather than interrupting their sequence, ask them if this is a good time. If they have too many interruptions or are told what to do, they can become resentful, defensive, and even rebellious.

Trust, fairness, and integrity are important, and if trust has been broken beyond repair they sometimes choose to walk away from relationships without looking back. The auditory-digital style person is extremely gifted at using logic to figure things out and in solving complex problems. These people share with the auditory style an enjoyment of words and, in particular, the specific meaning of words. They are organized, precise, thorough at handling details, and have a strong need for completion.

Put this all together and you can see that we are all different. And that's what makes our world so interesting. The more aware we are of the four communication styles, the more we can accept and respect differences and allow and honor people in being their true natural selves. The ultimate goal is to be able to celebrate those differences.

So relax … take a deep breath … and notice how you are starting to look at things from a different perspective. Having the flexibility to shift gears and know when to speak another person's language is truly a gift to them and to the universe.

What's your style?

Discover your own communication style by using the Communication Style Questionnaire and Score Sheet. Your two highest scores are the ones you use most often. Your lowest score will show you which communication style you are least comfortable with.

The Communications Style Questionnaire

For each of the following statements, please allocate a number to every phrase, ranking them from 4 to 1.

    4 = Closest to describing you
    3 = Next closest description
    2 = Somewhat describes you
    1 = Least descriptive of you

1. I make important decisions based on:
   ___ my gut feeling and comfort level
   ___ how the idea sounds to me
   ___ how it looks to me
   ___ precise review and study of the issues

2. During a disagreement, I am most likely to be influenced by:
   ___ the volume and tone of the other person's voice
   ___ whether or not I can see the other person's point of view
   ___ the logic and rationale of the other person's opinion
   ___ whether or not the other person is sensitive to my feelings

3. When communicating with others, what's important to me is:
   ___ the way I dress and look
   ___ sharing my feelings and experiences
   ___ knowing that the meaning of my words is understood
   ___ being heard and listened to

4. When someone is asking me an important question,
   I tend to:
   ___ listen carefully, then ask questions to ensure
       I understand
   ___ prefer time to think it over and to choose my
       words carefully
   ___ appreciate being given time to search inside
       for the answer
   ___ answer quickly, describing it in pictures

5. I would consider myself:
   ___ attuned to the sounds of my surroundings
   ___ able to easily make sense of new facts and data
   ___ sensitive and flexible in my relationships
   ___ creative and able to handle tremendous amounts
       of information quickly

6. People really know me best when they ...
   ___ can relate to what I'm feeling
   ___ can see my perspective
   ___ listen carefully to what I have to say and how
       it is said
   ___ are interested in the meaning of what I am
       communicating

7. When working on a project with other people, I am more
   likely to:
   ___ want to improve the process with my ideas
   ___ want to be part of the vision and planning process

___ want to sequence the events and put things
     in order

___ want to help build good solid relationships

8. When describing things to me:

    ___ showing it to me brings clarity

    ___ I can remember well just by listening

    ___ writing it down helps me to integrate it

    ___ presenting the facts in a logical way makes sense

9. In times of stress I am most challenged with ...

    ___ trusting people, situations, or concepts

    ___ being diplomatic, being too blunt and to the point

    ___ separating my feelings from what other people
        are feeling

    ___ being flexible and changing the timing of plans

10. I find it easy and natural to:

    ___ receive inner inspirations

    ___ tell where new ideas fit in

    ___ follow the direction of tried-and-true methods

    ___ organize and plan events

Calculate your score by using the score sheet found on the next two pages. Your highest score is your dominant communication style.

Visit: www.EveryDayChoicesCoaching.com for the online version of this questionnaire with automated calculation.

Step 1:

Copy your answers from the questionaire to the lines below.

Example:

1.

_4_	K
_3_	A
_1_	V
_2_	D

1.	2.	3.	4.	5.
——— K	——— A	——— V	——— A	——— A
——— A	——— V	——— K	——— D	——— D
——— V	——— D	——— D	——— K	——— K
——— D	——— K	——— A	——— V	——— V

6.	7.	8.	9.	10.
——— K	——— A	——— V	——— D	——— D
——— V	——— V	——— A	——— A	——— A
——— A	——— D	——— K	——— K	——— K
——— D	——— K	——— D	——— V	——— V

Step 2:

Copy your scores into the boxes that correspond to each letter.

Example:

	V	A	K	D
1	*1*	*3*	*4*	*2*

Your Scores:

	V	A	K	D
1				
2				
3				
4				
5				
6				
7				
8				
9				
10				

To make sure you've completed this score sheet correctly, tally your score. It should add up to 100. For example: K=29, V=27, D=24, A=20 TOTAL=100

The Communications Style Comparison Chart

	Visual	Auditory
Common characteristics	Sees a thought as a picture Memorizes by seeing Learns quickly High energy Easily bored Arrives, starts, and ends on time	Hears a thought as a sound or word Memorizes by hearing Quickly picks up new ideas Seems scattered Very private person Likes music and the sound of own voice
Commonly used words	See Look Appear View Show Imagine Crystallize	Hear Listen Sound Tune in/out Click Ring a bell Harmonize
Questions that engage each style	Do you see what I mean? Are you getting the picture? How does this look so far?	Does this sound OK? Tell me … Is this clicking with you? How can this be improved?
How they end a conversation	"See you later."	"Talk to you later."
Greatest challenges	**Flexibility**—easily becomes rigid if picture gets changed too fast **Impatience**—with details **Boredom**—with slow pace, too many words, or long meetings	**Diplomacy**—blunt, harsh, or too direct with words **Angry**—starts yelling if they feel they aren' being heard. Wants to argue his/her point **Interrupting**—has a hard time listening **Changes subjects** frequently
How to support the person	Provide an agenda Keep sessions short Color-code systems Use see-through containers Provide handouts Start and end on time Give ample time to change, postpone, or reschedule events	Provide an agenda Ask where person is at Avoid pressure Keep him/her on track Suggest tape-recording meetings or session Ensure feeling of being heard Break things down into small steps
Best team player position	Big picture visionary Planning stage Organizing Timing Project manager Leading—being seen	Idea and invention stage Leadership position Start of project Finishing a project—gets bored with the middle

Kinesthetic	Auditory-Digital
Feels a thought as a sensation	Senses a thought as a knowing
Memorizes by doing	Memorizes by steps or sequence
Needs time to get a feeling	Needs time to process information
Nurturing and supportive	Good problem solver
Likes group activities	Works best alone and uninterrupted
Loyal to family, friends, and employer	Strong "need to know" re: future
	Loves closure and completions
Feel	Sense
Touch	Experience
Touch base	Understand
Get hold of	Think
Comfortable	Process
Catch on	Decide
Play together	I know
How does this feel? Is this comfortable?	Is this making sense? Do you understand?
What have you learned from this situation?	What did you think about that?
Getting a handle on this?	Can you figure this out for me?
"Let's touch base soon."	"Bye."
Discernment—tends to be "emotional sponge" and absorb other people's feelings **Detachment**—from needing to fix or make situations better **Manipulation**—wants people and situations to change so everyone feels good	**Trust**—needs to know people, things, etc. can be trusted. If feels betrayed, it may be impossible to re-establish trust **Interruptions**—break the sequence, cause irritation, anger, resentment, or rebellion **Stubborn**—if told what to do. Ask
Provide an agenda	Provide an agenda
Use wording that is sensitive	Establish project timeline together
Ask person to share	Present things in a logical, rational way
Create a start date for project	"Ask" that things be done, rather than tell
Create an end date for project	Let person know they are in "personal control"
Provide time to decide and to process new ideas	Provide uninterrupted time alone
Include time for creativity, fun, play, and socializing	Ensure a sense of closure
Creative touches	Creative "what if" stage
Final touches	Project development
Quality control	Ensuring order and maintenance
Team rapport/morale	Complex problem solver
Details	Detail oriented
Decision making	Analyzer

Recommended Resources

Websites

1. **Law of Attraction Resources**
   www.lawofattractionresources.com

Order additional copies of this book and other Law of Attraction books, CDs, tapes, and other products.

2. **You Can Have It All**
   www.youcanhaveitall.com

My coaching website contains information about how to hire me for one-on-one coaching. As well, it contains many powerful articles about my Law of Attraction experiences.

3. **Law of Attraction Training Center**
   www.lawofattractiontrainingcenter.com

Learn how you can become a Certified Law of Attraction Practitioner and bring this message to your clients and audience. If you're a coach, therapist, seminar speaker, bodyworker, teacher, nurse, minister, chiropractor, or other helping professional looking for a specialty niche or "hot topic," then this is the right place for you.

4. **Abraham-Hicks.com**
   www.abraham-hicks.com

Esther and Jerry Hicks have been teaching the Law of Attraction for years. They have a wide variety of books, tapes, and CDs available through their website. Their weekly and/or monthly tape or CD subscription is highly recommended.

5. **Images of One**
   www.imagesofone.com

David Cameron is one of the few living "in-depth" writers on the Law of Attraction, spiritual enlightenment, self-knowledge, and actualization. He is one of my favorite mentors. His books are all downloadable, and he has created interactive software that actually guides you into deeper understanding. This is metaphysics "in blue jeans"— practical, understandable, and transforming.

6. **Sacred Science Institute**
   www.sacredscience.com

This website is a portal for many ancient writings that contain references to the Law of Attraction.

7. ***The Kybalion***
   http://kybalion.home.att.net/kybalion.html

The Hermetic Philosophy of Ancient Egypt and Greece. One of the Universal Laws recognized by the ancients is the Law of Attraction.

8. **Summum: Sealed Except to the Open Mind**
   www.summum.us/philosophy/kybalion.shtml

This book rewrites the information found in *The Kybalion* in a manner more appropriate for our modern era. It also presents new material not found in *The Kybalion*, thus giving a complete and more in-depth outline of an age-old philosophy.

Books

1. Law of Attraction Michael J. Losier

You may not be aware of it, but a very powerful force is at work in your life. It's called the Law of Attraction and right now it's attracting people, jobs, and relationships to your life—not all of them good! If your life feels as if it's turned south and taken on the characteristics of a bad soap opera, it's time to pick up this book

- Paperback: 108 pages
- Publisher: Michael J. Losier; (February 2003)
- ISBN: 0973224002

2. Excuse Me, Your Life Is Waiting: The Astonishing Power of Feelings Lynn Grabhorn

This book picks up where most positive-thinking books leave off, giving us the rather startling new information that every moment of our lives is governed by our EMOTIONS, not by luck, or hard work, or circumstance, or good thoughts, or visualization.

- Paperback: 309 pages
- Publisher: Hampton Roads Publishing Company; (March 1, 2003)
- ISBN: 1571743812

3. Think and Grow Rich Napoleon Hill

This book has influenced millions of people in recent years and is the all-time bestseller in the field.

- Hardcover: 288 pages Publisher: Ballantine Books;
- Reissue edition (November 1, 1990)
- ISBN: 0449214923

4. Thought Vibration: The Law of Attraction in the Thought World William Walker Atkinson

This book is one of the first modern-day publications to explain the Law of Attraction. Written in 1906, some of the chapter titles include: Law of Attraction in the Thought World; Thought-Waves & Their Power of Reproduction; A Talk About the Mind; Mind Building; Secret of the Will; and How to Become Immune to Injurious Thought Attraction.

- Paperback: 144 pages
- Publisher: Kessinger Publishing; (March 1, 1997)
- ISBN: 1564596605

5. The Science of Getting Rich or Financial Success Through Creative Thought Wallace D. Wattles

This is one of my favorites. Throughout this book, originally published in 1910, Wallace Wattles focuses on the power of thought and shows how to use willpower for achieving goals. Pointing out that life is a self-fulfilling prophecy, he advocates the purposeful direction of thought and action. Because all of life is connected, the author discourages competition and urges the reader to create value instead. By getting rich in a creative way, no harm is done to other people; on the contrary, others will benefit from the inspiration that comes from the successful person. Arguing strongly in the tradition of 19th-century art and social critic John Ruskin that there is no wealth but life, Wattles, with this work, created the ancestor of many a modern self-help and personal finance book.

- Paperback: 108 pages
- Publisher: Iceni Books; (January 1, 2002)
- ISBN: 1587360942

About the Author

It's Rebecca Hanson's own history with the Law of Attraction that makes her ideally suited to teach others about this universal law.

She first learned about the Law of Attraction in 1999. Her grasp of its workings was so great that she soon attracted everything she needed to know and have to achieve her dream of living by the ocean. She moved from the Canadian prairies to the island city of Victoria, British Columbia, on Canada's west coast.

After decades of being a homemaker and raising five children, Rebecca added "successful businesswoman" to her résumé. As the owner of seven successful businesses—Aurora Websites, TeleClass International Services Inc. and its three subsidiary companies (Telephone Bridge Services, TeleClass Registration Systems, and Corporate TeleLeader Training), the Law of Attraction Training Center, and You Can Have It All Coaching—Rebecca is a testament to the power of the Law of Attraction. She started her first business at the age of 51. Now she has satisfied clients throughout North America, New Zealand, and the United Kingdom.

Rebecca is the mother of five beautiful children, and an ever-increasing number of grandchildren. She lives in Victoria, British Columbia, Canada.

Glossary

Alignment:
When you're feeling good, happy, joyful, and positive, you're in alignment with all you were created to be and do; you send strong vibrational signals into the atmosphere. These signals attract more positive situations so you can feel even more wonderful.

Contrast:
Contrast is any external event that doesn't feel good. Contrast is a prompt that something is unfinished or unexamined. It's a neutral term for the experience of external events that awaken a desire for change.

Core values:
Our core values are deeply embedded values that give us guidance by producing good feelings when we honor them and negative feelings when we don't. Some core values include honesty, kindness, loyalty, compassion, and goodness.

Deliberate attraction:
Deliberate attraction is a simple three-step process for using the power of the Law of Attraction to get more of what you want and less of what you don't.

Step A: Get clarity about the outcome you desire

Step B: Raise your vibration to match your desire

Step C: Allow what you've asked for to arrive

Inner Being:

Your Inner Being is the unseen spark of divine life within you. It's your True Self, Pure Love, Goodness, God, Universe, or Higher Power.

Law of Attraction:

The Law of Attraction tells us that we become magnets for whatever we give our attention to—whether wanted or unwanted. It doesn't know the difference between remembering the past, observing the present, or imagining the future. It only responds to our current vibration.

Magnet:

When a piece of steel is placed next to a lodestone—a natural magnet in the Earth—all the atoms in the steel line up so that all the positively charged atoms face one direction and all the negatively charged ones face the opposite direction. This is called alignment. As we become more and more aligned with who we are and why we're here, based on what feels good, we become powerful magnets. We attract everything we need to know, say, or do. Each of our endeavors is successful and brings us joy. Similarly, when we surround ourselves with others who are in alignment, our own magnetism is strengthened.

Meter:

Every person has an internal meter—feelings and emotions—that is individually calibrated for specific purposes. Your meter is for you. It's in alignment with all you were created to be and do.

Resistance:
Resistance stands in the way of you obtaining your desires. Two great hindrances to allowing what you've asked for to arrive are doubts and fears.

Scripts:
Scripts are different from business plans in that they arise from our imagination and produce a total body, mind, and soul experience. Once the script is written, your plan is on autopilot. You can write a script for any event or topic. Every detail matters, however. Choose your words carefully and describe what feels good for you.

Law of Attraction T-Tool™:
You can get quick results by using the Law of Attraction T-Tool™ to gain clarity about any subject. When you briefly examine it by writing down what doesn't feel good, and have the intention to change it, you're actually clearing away an unwanted vibration and replacing it with a wanted one.

Vibrations:
Your thoughts, feelings, emotions, and moods (positive and negative) send a range of vibrations (like sound waves) into the atmosphere. These vibrations act like big magnets and attract, draw, or pull toward you the people, events, opportunities, etc. that are a "vibrational match" to the vibrations you're emitting. The Law of Attraction responds to every vibration you emit.

Frequently Asked Questions

1. How is the Law of Attraction different from "positive thinking?"

While "positive thinking" focuses on only positive things, the Law of Attraction encourages you to examine events that feel negative for several reasons. The negative feeling lets you know that something you are thinking about or observing is not in alignment with your desire.

Ignoring negative feelings doesn't really change your vibration—you are still offering a negative vibration, even when you're not paying attention to it. This usually causes the negative event to increase in intensity until you *must* give it attention.

Negative feelings, if examined briefly, can be turned into positive desire statements. This allows you to offer a purer positive vibration.

2. What's the scientific explanation for how the Law of Attraction works?

Everything that exists vibrates. On a subatomic level, the protons and neutrons (elements of the atom) are really microscopic packets of energy bursts. These energy bursts keep the atoms in a state of constant motion (vibration), although we can see this movement only through the most powerful microscope.

Our thoughts contain energy (vibrations). The effects of our thoughts can be observed:

In our body, where our thoughts evoke certain emotions that cause glands to secrete chemicals or hormones. These, in turn, cause us to feel either good or bad.

In our environment, where our thoughts send vibrational signals into the atmosphere, much like radio signals, that draw to us people, events, opportunities, and things. These match the vibrational frequency of our thoughts.

3. I've had negative thoughts for so long. Will I be able to turn my life around? How long will it take?

The Law of Attraction is not "keeping score" of how long you thought negatively; it responds right away to your shift in vibration. How long it will take to notice that the majority of your thoughts are positive is up to you. There is no "standard" amount of time. I was 51 years old before I discovered the effects my thoughts were having on my life. I think it took me about 18 months to feel like the majority of my thoughts were more positive than negative—but I was coming from a very, very low vibration.

4. Is it possible to attract something I didn't ask for (e.g., a business setback)?

You may not have consciously asked for the setback. However, the Law of Attraction *is* responding to some forgotten, ignored, or subconscious vibration. And this is one way to get you to pay attention to that vibration. Once you acknowledge the operation of a vibration of fear, doubt, or disbelief, you can decide to change that vibration into one of trust, belief, or action. All it takes is a decision to choose a thought that feels better.

5. Will there ever be a time when I only attract good or wonderful things into my world?

No. We need the contrast of "not-so-wonderful" experiences to bring us to the point of making a decision. Without contrast we would become passive. The more contrast we experience, the more clarity we can derive about what would feel better, thus creating more and more experiences that feel good.

6. Is it possible to attract a specific person, project, job, or business into my life?

It's possible to focus so intently we orchestrate events that bring us together with specific people. However, it may not be an enjoyable experience. If the other party wasn't looking for you or your business, the experience may feel like an intrusion or manipulation to them. It's better to get clear about the *essence* of your desire and let the Law of Attraction bring to you people, projects, or business that are a closer match with your vibration.

7. I've completed the Law of Attraction T-Tool™, but I'm still not clear about what kind of job or business I would love. What else can I do?

Take a good look at what you wrote on the "I do want …" side of your Law of Attraction T-Tool™ and circle the most important statement. Now, underline the most important word in that statement—this word represents the "essence" of what you want.[1] Focusing on the essence of what you do want, write a script starting with the phrase: "If I had my way …"

You can also ask the Universe, God, your Higher Power, to bring you clarity in ways you will easily notice. Sometimes I pray, "I don't know what I need to know, but I really need to know it." Remember: When you ask the question, the answer *will* come.

8. How can I get my co-worker to become more positive?

While you can't force someone to be positive, you can create a cheerful atmosphere in which they may find it easier to be upbeat. Ask yourself how it feels when others think poorly of you. Then imagine how it feels when your friends or colleagues think you are wonderful. Which thought feels better? When we choose to focus on the positive aspects in others, we allow them to respond in the most positive ways. When we choose to focus *only* on the positive aspects in others, we keep our own vibration high.

9. I want out of my present job so badly. How can I speed things up so I can quit?

The best way to shorten the time spent in a negative situation is to focus on all the positives you can. If you can't find a single positive aspect of your present job, just act as if you *are* working in a fun place. The Law of Attraction doesn't know the difference between remembering the past, observing the present, or imagining the future. So if you act as if you like your job, you'll either attract a different set of situations in that job or you'll soon find yourself working in a new place that feels great!

Remember, your thoughts and feelings today are creating your tomorrow. So, if you keep noticing what you don't like about your current job, you'll attract another job with a similar set of challenges.

10. What do I need to do to make this work for me?

Just start working the Law of Attraction formula. Get started by identifying an area of your life or business with which you are unhappy, then ask yourself, "So, if I don't want this, what do I want?"

Remember: The Law of Attraction Formula is a simple three-step process:

Step A: Get clarity about the outcome you desire by using the Law of Attraction T-Tool™.

Step B: Raise your vibration to match your desire. Use the three phrases:

"I'm in the process of ..."

"The Law of Attraction is in the process of ..."

"I love it when ..."

Step C: Allow what you've asked for to arrive. Believe and receive.

Formula for Desired Experience:
A + B + C = DE (Desired Experience)

1 This technique comes from Lynn Ahearn, certified Law of Attraction practitioner and speaker.

NOTES

Order more copies of this book!

Visit www.lawofattractionresources.com
to see the full list of complementary
Law of Attraction products,
including CDs and TeleClasses.

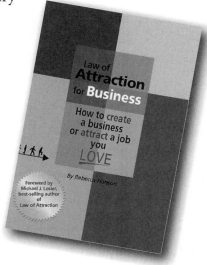

Your name

Address

City   Province/State

Country   Postal Code/Zip

Telephone

Email

Fill out this form, including the next page, cut out and submit.

Book Title	Price (each)	Quantity	Sub Total
Law of Attraction for Business	US$18.95 CDN$24.95		

Tax (Canadian residents only) GST (7%)		
Shipping		
First Book	US/CDN$7.00	
Each additional book	US/CDN$5.00	
TOTAL		

Credit Card Payment:

☐ VISA ☐ MasterCard ☐ AMEX ☐ Discover

Card number _____

Name on Card _____ Exp. Date (m/y) _____

Fax orders: (use this form) 1-561-828-3786

Telephone orders: Call toll-free 1-866-594-7303

Secure online orders: www.lawofattractionresources.com

U.S. money order:
Law of Attraction Resources
c/o Rebecca Hanson
777 Fort Street, #110
Victoria, BC Canada
V8W 1G9

Email orders: orders@lawofattractionresources.com

Volume or reseller orders: visit www.lawofattractionresources.com